My eyes darted to my father's face, asking him the question: "What happened here?" The words my young mind could not articulate were, "Why is this place so forlorn, dirty, and broken?"

My father squeezed my hand, answering without speaking. "It's okay. I'm here with you. Everything is fine."

My tiny insides churned with uncertainty, but I trusted I was safe with my dad.

It Was Always You and Me:

The Story of a Father
and the Love He Shared
with His Daughter

All the best!

Diane

XOXO

By Diane DiProspero Cook

Copyright ©2021 by Diane DiProspero Cook

ISBN 978-1-7377071-0-3

Copyright ©2021

Library of Congress Control Number: 2021920260

Cover Design: Elle J. Rossi

Layout: Suzanne Blessing

Publishing Coordinator: Elly Stevens

* * * * * * * *

Printed in the United States of America

Dedication

For Joseph, my dad,
with all the love my heart can hold.

For Anna, Millie, Tom, Grandma Angelina,
and Grandpa Tony.
Without you, where would I be?

For Rick and Shannon and Jaimee,
my loves, and the beat in my heart.

I love you all.

*You are more than your thoughts, your body,
or your feelings.*

*You are a swirling vortex of limitless potential who is
here to shake things up and create something new
that the universe has never seen.*

— Dr. Richard Bartlett

* * * * * * *

*The two most important days in your life
are the day you are born
and the day you find out why.*

— Mark Twain

Table of Contents

Preface

Like a flower slowly blooming, my life—with all its mysteries revealed—has unfolded in front of my eyes. The how and why of my life, the circumstances surrounding my arrival in this world, and ending up with such a wonderful family were surely examples of serendipity. Eventually, I even found my biological siblings, which was truly a miracle! Over the past few years, I have watched my memories in my dreams. I've written with what feels like divine inspiration the memories etched into my consciousness. This snapshot of my life extends beyond the scope of my imagination even though I recall the events of my life in exquisite detail.

My memoir has been written with the help of God whose plan for me, and really for each of us, reveals itself slowly throughout our lives. This is my humble attempt to chronicle my story in the hope that it helps you navigate your own life.

My story is not just my own. It is about birth and the miracle of life. As everyone does, I continue to struggle and face sadness. From a place of cheerful innocence and with my own "cheeky" humor, I've come to an understanding that it doesn't matter how we got to where we are now, but only that we endure, love, and grow.

I'm amazed by the memories I have, even from the womb. Scientific evidence suggests this is a very real phenomenon. How else could a baby at birth recognize the sound of its own mother's voice? When my oldest daughter, Shannon, was born, I left my room to go find her in the maternity ward. From the midst of the sea of newborn infants, I walked up to and correctly identified my daughter. I knew instinctively she was mine.

I deliberately planned to have two children, because I grew up as an only child. Although my life was great, and I was blessed beyond measure to be an only adopted child, I wanted my daughter to have a sibling. Not having a sibling was the one thing that often made me feel "different" and I often wished I had one.

If I'd never found my biological siblings on my biological father's side of the family, and my sister Karen from my biological mother's side, I would have been okay.

But I'm getting ahead of myself. Despite being cocooned and sheltered by my loving adoptive family, from my parents to my extended Italian family, I was not always happy. I still grew and thrived through it all, but there were issues, as you will see. My parents instilled and inspired me through their examples of love, persistence, faith in God, and family traditions. Those things enabled me to cope with just about anything life threw at me. From observing their struggles, I, too, learned to cope through grace and humor.

If I am to be honest, the most important and truest beauty of my life was found in the mutual and enormous love I shared with my dad. He and I were blessed to experience and revel in that love, one even his death cannot destroy. This story is largely his as much as it is mine. He was my hero who not only guided and loved me beyond measure but showed me loyalty, love, goodness, and strength through his character, anchoring and sustaining our entire family and proving that love can indeed triumph overall.

I hope this story resonates with you and makes you more alert and open to life's wonders and miracles.

Me—Diane Frances, at 9 months old, 1962.

Prologue: The Perfect Day

We could make it together

The further from here, girl, the better

Where the air is fresh and clean

Oh, my Candida

—Tony Orlando and Dawn

On the perfect day, I got a respite from all the craziness. Tiny ribbons of clouds decorated robin's egg blue skies. The sun shone overhead, its rays warming my skin. My mother, wondrously or, at least, mostly clear-headed for a change, actually smiled and seemed happy. My dad was happy. I was happy. We were all together.

At ten years old, I was still in the magical stage where full consciousness hasn't really emerged. Life happened to me at that point, as I didn't have full control of the reins or the cognizance to really make things happen *for* me. I soaked things in, but I remained at the mercy of my family and the world around me. Their routines were my routines, their lives governed mine. Things were still hazy at ten. I didn't really know or care how the bills were paid. I didn't care about inevitable things like death or taxes or anything much except myself. My world consisted of eating, sleeping, going to school, and hanging with my friends.

On the imperfect days which were most of them, my mom screamed from her bedroom, convulsing from all the pills she'd ingested. Constantly wailing, she called me horrid names for hours on end while I was left home alone with her.

What else do you do as a ten-year-old? You turn up your music in your room, shut your door, and pray for it to end. At least, that's what I did.

Sometimes I called my dad, who worked a second job as a bartender, but he couldn't leave work to help me. Sometimes I called my aunt to come and rescue me if she wasn't working herself. If she wasn't available, I had another aunt I could call.

This day wasn't like that though. The world swirled around me, and I rode on the clouds of parental happiness surrounding me. Colors twisted and danced. We were going to the State Fair, just like any other family.

The weather was hot, ninety degrees, and the fair was crowded. We walked among others in the crowd, my dad holding my hand, my mom talking, not yelling for a change.

I smelled the fair food. You know the things I'm talking about. The sweetness of cotton candy chased by the aroma of roasting peanuts. The next vendor offered a variety of fried foods, and I smelled the grease before I felt it on my skin as I walked by.

Past the food, we came to the stalls where the animals were kept, some with ribbons on their nameplates, telling me they'd won. At ten, you don't know what the fate of that prize pig is, you only hope you, too, are a winner. That day the only things that mattered to me were the colors of the ribbons, the sounds of grunting and snorting animals, and the smell. That and the feeling of pure joy and anticipation. It was as if I was in a kind of paradise. Who knew what adventure was in store for me?

A man pushed past us, spilling a little of the cheap beer out of a clear plastic cup. It seemed like everyone who was old enough drank something with alcohol in it.

Women sold cheap jewelry made to look expensive. They called to us as we walked past, but we did not heed their cries. There were tickets and rides, some where I didn't quite reach the mark indicating how tall one must be to endure the terror and, in some cases, real danger. Still, I heard the bells, the gleeful screams of the passengers, the motors running in the background. I smelled the fuel for the generators, the exhaust cloying and comforting at the same time.

Other kids were there with their mothers and fathers, too. We were just a normal family at the fair.

The horror of my mother's prescription drug addiction and the constant verbal abuse that went with it disappeared for those precious hours. It didn't matter that money was tight or that this event was a rare, infrequent outing among few other elusive ones. I was with my dad, and I knew I was safe and loved.

The time for the evening performance neared, and we headed for the stage area. Tony Orlando and Dawn came out on the stage to perform. They waved to the crowd. His black mustache rode his lip like a caterpillar that would never transform into a beautiful butterfly, never have a life of its own.

My father spun me around to the music as they started to sing:

> *Candida, we could make it together,*
> *The farther from here, girl, the better,*
> *Where the air is fresh and clean,*
> *Oh, my Candida,*
> *Just take my hand and I'll lead ya.*

Time stood still. The music ended and my dad took me to one of the jewelry stands. He bought me a glass heart necklace with a red rose. The vendor engraved my name on the back. "Diane."

I wanted that day to last, not because of the fair or all the things there. I wanted to stay because I felt safe and loved. Life was good that day.

It was a perfect day.

Most of my days, even then, weren't perfect. But the first chapter of my life started with another perfect day.

That was the day my parents got the call, the one that changed everything for all of us.

Part One

Not flesh of my flesh, nor bone of my bone,

but still miraculously, my own.

Never forget for a single minute,

you didn't grow under my heart,

but in it.

— Elle Cosimance

Chapter One: The Call

I came into this world on a Friday. Friday, August 31, 1962, just 26 days after Marilyn Monroe's apparent suicide. I was only a couple of years old when the Cuban Missile Crisis began, and the world narrowly escaped a nuclear war. Just over a year later, President John F. Kennedy was assassinated.

The Universe, the cosmos, was spinning all around, as it does and as it will. My biological mother, Rose, grew up in a large home on Rochester's west side, along with her aunts and uncles, and her sickly and very strict Italian father.

Finding herself pregnant a second time, after having given up a baby girl seven years prior, thirty-year-old Rose was ashamed and alone again. Her mom died of cancer when she was just eleven, and rumor had it her uncle and father were relentlessly cruel to her regarding the position she once again found herself in. This cruelty precipitated mental anguish so great that she suffered several nervous breakdowns. She had to be hospitalized several times in her life for severe anxiety and depression.

But I didn't know that then. In utero, I was spinning, being created inside of her. I often wonder how growing inside the centrifuge of her womb laden with a chemical cocktail of hormones laced with grief, regret, anxiety, and fear impacted my own development. Was this stressful environment imprinted, literally into my DNA?

I remember glimpses, whether real or imagined, of being in utero. I have a memory, dreamlike in nature, of floating and hearing typing. I believe that memory happened while I was growing inside my mother, Rose. I do know that my mother was a secretary at the Simon-Germanow factory in Rochester, NY.

I never expressed this out loud, afraid of the looks people would have given me or what they would believe about me. But I know I possessed a type of conscious, awareness of something happening around me. Fast forward to my birth, a baby thrust into the cold and the light from my nine-month home. The crying and the doctor's slap to induce breathing as I was pushed out into the world? Of those events, I haven't the scarcest consciousness.

I was born at 10 a.m., or so my parents told me. Whether Rose held me or even saw me, I do not know. I do know I was placed in a foster home for the first six weeks of my life.

Sometime between the fifth and eighth of October, as tensions were building in Cuba, my parents got what came to be known as "The Call."

IT WAS ALWAYS YOU AND ME

I heard the story many times growing up, but as is often the case with these things, the details have gotten fuzzy.

This was a short, typed account by my mother of the day they got "the call" to adopt me. I heard the story so many times growing up, and my parents always made me feel so special, wanted, and loved. These few typed paragraphs were among a whole folder that my mother meticulously kept about all my milestones, illnesses, first words, cute things she thought I said and did...it was in a folder she titled, "Forget-me-Nots"!

My mother Anna, her twin sister Frances, my Aunt Millie, and my grandmother were all at a beauty shop that belonged to my Aunt Eva.

In reality, they were at my Uncle Al's house. He was my dad's "baby brother."

Eva and Al had three boys, Joe, Al, and David, (who would become my three very close cousins, to this day and later their wives, too, Lauri, Diane, and Peggy), and so my aunt worked out of their house in a "shop" connected to their kitchen. Her customers were mostly friends and family members but there were enough of them that she earned a little extra money on the side.

To adopt me, my parents had gone through extensive background and mandatory health checks. Random home inspections had been conducted, and persistent questions by social workers, one by the name of Miss Hickey, were answered. She'd regularly give my mother parenting scenarios to test her probable reactions as if anyone can, with any accuracy, declare what their future behavior will be concerning their children.

I remember the story clearly because my mother would share every detail whenever she told the tale of my adoption.

That day, she sat in the shop with her hair all rolled up in black "pinchy" rollers, pink cosmetic tape holding her wayward bangs to her forehead.

Both my grandmother and my aunt sat under hairdryers in the corner, magazines in hand. Early sixties music drifted from the speakers, spicing the dish of beauty-store gossip.

A ringing telephone interrupted all of that.

My Aunt Eva, untethered by either hairdryer or curlers, answered.

Her face lit up, and immediately she handed the phone to my mother.

"The baby is ready!" she said. "They have a baby girl for you, and they want you to come now, Ann!"

The dryer hoods were lifted, and everyone started to talk excitedly at once.

"What's going on?" my grandmother demanded to know.

"What?" from Aunt Millie.

"What? The baby?" came another exclamation.

"No, really?"

"Yes, really, right now," my Aunt Eva told them.

My mother grabbed the phone and spoke briefly to the person on the other end of the line.

She couldn't remember exactly what she said. She was trying to process it all, but one thing did register.

She hung up the phone, tore the rollers from her hair, and freed her bangs from the tape on her forehead.

Then she dialed my dad's number.

"Joe, the baby is ready for us. I'm at Eva's. Come and get me. They said we need to go, now!"

Once she hung up, there were tears and shrieks of laughter.

My parents were coming to get me and to rescue me. My new home, and my destiny, were waiting for me.

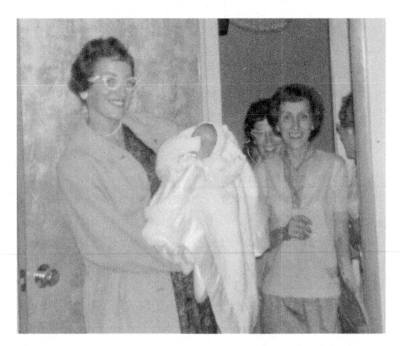

My homecoming from adoption proceedings, as I was brought into my new Marilou Drive home at 6 weeks old. My mom, Anna (Baldo) DiProspero, holding me, her twin, Aunt Frances Dee, to the right. Behind them, to the left, Mom's oldest sister, Aunt Millie (Maggio) and Grandma Angelina Baldo, far right corner.

Chapter Two: Telephones and Angels Come Calling

My mom sat on one of the two easy chairs in our living room. Between them stood a marble-topped mahogany end table with a tall, ornate lamp on it. The shade was covered in plastic, to protect it from the Parliament® cigarette ever-present between the fingers of her hand.

A "silent butler," as this relic from this era was known, also occupied the table. It had a smallish, oblong base with ornate roses and flowers decorating its top. When she pressed a long handle, the lid opened to reveal a square receptacle where the cigarette butts were snuffed and deposited. The container would eventually fill with the nasty leavings, and she would remove it from its place and empty it into the trash pail.

Ann's hair was short, her neck razored, the sides pin curled, teased up a bit. Her bangs were straight and short over her "Batwoman glasses," characteristic of the 1950s and 1960s. Typically, she wore a white or other pastel cotton-short sleeved button-down blouse with a round Peter Pan collar, ironed crisp and flawless. "Pedal-pusher" pants now commonly called "capris," either in a seer-sucker pale pastel shade or sometimes a fun plaid, polka-dot, or stripe completed her outfit. She held the long twisted, curly phone cord in the hand opposite her cigarette.

"ID 7-6707," or "Fairview 8-5504," she would mouth out loud as she dialed.

I remember these things clearly. I sat in awe, observing all her habits, her ways, her manner of dress, my large brown eyes staring in wonder at the littlest things. I silently observed everything she and my dad did, those memories coded and burned into my brain.

I was often morose as a child. I was skinny and even underweight, knobby-kneed with pin-straight, silky blackish hair, cut short. My mother complained that even a "permanent wave" out of a box would not curl that hair.

My obvious sadness and seriousness were due to my mom's illness. It always seemed like, as much as I was cherished and given attention, my mom was truly at the center of the universe of our family's consciousness. We were all constantly attuned to her ever-changing moods and her ups and downs, due to not only her depression but to her prescription addiction. I felt laden with the heavy burden of silence and secrecy about her issues, far too heavy for a young child to have to bear.

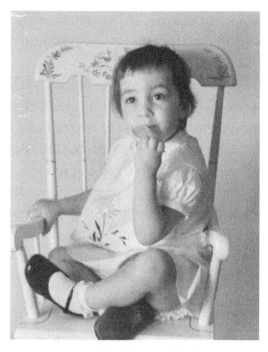

Me at about age 2 or 2½. There's a similar photo with a telephone where I look like I am hollering at someone. (I was ALWAYS a talker and "communicator" from a very young age!) In this photo I have my trusty pacifier. My mother told me she couldn't break me of that habit until I was about 4!

My eyes were dark brown and overly large, often with dark circles under them.

Sometimes sickly, I often had severe nose bleeds that would start with me bleeding spontaneously in my sleep. I'd wake up soaked in blood and terrified.

Unable to stop the bleeding on her own, my mom would rush me to the Emergency Room to have my nose packed with gauze. My dad would return at 2 or 3 a.m. from his job tending the bar he and my uncle owned and discover all the lights on in the house, and blood all over my pillows. He would know to go to St. Mary's hospital in the city where he knew my mom and I would be waiting.

I outgrew those horrible nose bleeds. I had a weak blood vessel in my nose, and after two painful cauterizations, these horrible episodes finally ended.

I also had seemingly never-ending bouts with stomach viruses which often left me retching up to 12 hours at a time, all through my grade school and part of my high school years. On top of all these things, being born a girl, evolving into adolescence obviously brought on menstruation. From the time I can remember, I suffered horribly, and nothing was ever easy. I would become terribly anemic and have no energy. I was considered "healthy," yet not so much all at the same time, and between all these chronic health issues, and severe allergies, I was also trying to be a normal teenager, get good grades, be with friends and deal (secretly) with all my mother's issues, too.

I also suffered from endless throat infections and even bouts of hives. Eventually, after a case of severe tonsillitis at age 20, my tonsils were finally removed. This brought me a measure of relief and renewed health.

I didn't smile a lot. Despite my physical struggles, I worried about my mother and her physical and mental state. Many times, even as a child; I felt it was up to me to take care of her and to "fix" her, although, sadly, I could not.

Despite that, to me, my mother vacillated between looking and acting like either Donna Reed or Annette

Funicello, my Aunt Millie called her "Dr. Jekyll and Mr. Hyde" because of her rapid personality and mood swings. These mood changes resulted in large part because she sought to suppress severe headaches and assuage depression by using prescription pills, which, in turn, triggered depression.

I was constantly trying to make sense of her many quirks, facets, phobias, insecurities, and her unpredictable and volatile nature. Often confused and sad, and I would retreat into my inner world. I did not realize until later that I was coding these memories as if they were a kind of lifeblood I needed to preserve for some reason. My brain was like an old-fashioned tape recorder, taking it all in, and keeping it.

Fairview 8, ID 7, Beverly 9 were the old telephone call ID numbers indicating the first three digits of a telephone number and were always followed by the numbers. These "area code phrases" indicated various geographical pockets within Rochester, NY.

My mom would sit, smoke, and chat almost daily to her sisters, my grandmother, or her sisters-in-law, catching up on daily news and family events. There are baby pictures of me adamantly scolding someone on my first toy, a dial-up phone, probably mimicking my mom's conversations.

When I was around 14, my aunt and uncle returned from a three-week European vacation in which they traveled to 9 countries in 21 days. They brought me a beautiful bracelet with a charm replica of each country that they visited. That was not my favorite gift, though. They also brought me a small white phone, shaped like a clam. It flipped open to reveal a push-button and interior dial. That phone was the envy of all my pre-pubescent friends, who not only didn't have a phone in their bedrooms but surely didn't possess an "Italian flip phone."

After that, I spent hours holed up in my bedroom, whether my mom was sick or well, chatting with all my girlfriends on my cherished and unique phone from Italy.

We never moved. We lived in the same house on Marilou Drive, but life moved on. The peddle-pusher pants disappeared, and rotary phones became a thing of the past.

My husband and I got our first van, which came with one of the first cellular phones, what a perk! The problem was we had no idea what to do with it. The phone itself was as big as a small baseball bat, and my husband, Rick solemnly told me, "This is for emergencies, and if you need to call 911!"

I never did use that phone, thankfully, but it sat perched in between the seats "just in case."

After that came the first small-sized flip cell phones. We made sure Dad, Mom, and Aunt Millie, and Uncle Tom all had them just in case of those same kinds of emergencies.

The phones evolved, the styles, and our lives moved along with them. Our family, our times together, all the conversations, the chats, the good times, and the bad times simply moved from one type of phone to the next. My mom and dad grew older as the phones got newer and more advanced.

What I wasn't prepared for and never would be, would be the other calls, from new phones or old phones, the calls every life brings but the ones everyone dreads.

These included the call my mother took when I was just seven years old informing her that her dad, who was in Florida at the time, had suffered a heart attack.

The call just before I raced to the hospital for my mother's emergency open-heart surgery after her angiogram went wrong while I was pregnant with my daughter, Jaimee.

The call that my aunt had passed away from her battle with Alzheimer's just ten days before my older daughter's wedding, and the call the night my mother passed away from heart failure. That night, I had to call my dad at his house and tell him Mom had passed away.

But the call I will never forget, the one that hurt the most and changed my life forever, was the call that I received on April 28, 2017.

"Mrs. Cook?"

"Yes?"

"This is Strong Memorial Hospital. I'm the attending physician for your father, Joseph DiProspero." It was around midnight. "I'm sorry to tell you, but there's been an incident. You need to come to the hospital as soon as you can."

But I'll get to that. All of it. For now, I need to tell you about the rest of our journey, that of my father and me.

Chapter Three: Childhood

My childhood was an interesting one from the start. From a young age, I was told I was adopted by my parents. They never wanted the fact that I was adopted to affect me, or for me to hear it from someone else, and thought if neighborhood kids or school kids knew my story, they might taunt me. I think they feared the meanness inherent in many children who might say things like: "Those are not your *real* parents."

From the time I could understand what adoption was, my parents were honest with me. I think I was around 5 when they explained it the first time. I'm not sure what I thought or felt then, but I just accepted the words they used to describe my situation. How could I not? At that point in my life, I knew nothing else.

They added detail to the story as I grew and answered any questions I had as my awareness deepened. They always stressed to me how much they loved and wanted me, and how I was "chosen," which made me feel special and cared for.

Even early in my life, I felt a deep responsibility to make them proud of me because of this. I was like a sponge, impressionable and observing of everything around me. I learned from every story and every example told and shown to me about my family's love. Even when I was a child, their actions were not lost on me.

I remember these stories and their examples, and while they may seem random as I look back, they truly shaped me. My mind imprinted them and framed them positively.

One example is my grandmother, who I remember spoke of such hunger and abject poverty growing up that she sometimes would faint from lack of food. She sometimes did things like hold up a ripe peach and simply marvel at it. I never forgot this.

Why would she marvel at a peach and why do I remember that moment so well? It showed me her deep gratitude for even the simplest things. It taught me to marvel at them, and not to take anything for granted. It taught me that in the worst of times, we can always find things to smile about, be grateful for, and celebrate.

I spent many afternoons as a child, during summers, holidays, and weekends cooking and baking with my grandmother. She would make a special Italian dessert called "spfinge" (basically, a dough dumpling fried in a big pot of oil) generally, in March around the feast of St. Joseph, my dad's patron Saint.

I would watch as she dropped balls of this dough batter into the hot oil. They would twist and turn, rolling, popping, and dancing. She would laugh and laugh at the sight, which seemed to amuse her so. Pretty soon the sight of my rotund grandma getting so silly over something so small, would start me laughing, too. These lessons, and her enjoyment of life in general, helped me survive the darkest days of my life.

My Uncle Tom was the same: part prankster, part silly inventor, sweet, kind, and generous to a fault, he also grew up with almost nothing. When I was older, I learned the only thing he dreamed of as a boy was owning his own bicycle, and it broke my heart that he never did because his family was too poor.

Because of these many examples of love, kindness, and generosity that surrounded me, I understood how blessed I was. "Those to whom much is given, much is expected," is what my inner mantra always has been.

As a child, I can remember teachers telling my parents I was creative and extremely verbal. I have always been a rather avid reader as well. Words, in a sense, saved me. The desire to express myself and to use them to process everything around me helped me survive what was next.

This is how I survived my dysfunctional mother; I spent most of my time after school alone in my bedroom. I spent many long weekday evenings, weekends, and late nights isolated while my dad was moonlighting at his second job. He was paddling as fast as he could, to keep our family afloat, since my mom was always too sick to go to work or even be a mother to me.

l read a lot, I cried a lot, I relied on my extended family to help me out. My aunt and uncle and my grandmother, and my mom's twin when she was well, all helped care for me when my mother was troubled, and things seemed the bleakest. I escaped to friends' and neighbors' houses whenever possible.

When push came to shove, I always had a family to rely on.

I am so thankful.

Chapter Four: Mama Dearest

When she was well, my mother often said that the two most important questions at the end of our lives are: "Am I loved?" and "Did I love well?"

The answer to the first question is often determined by how we practice the second in our lives. Certain aspects are out of our control. For instance, you may inherit a family that is unloving and does not teach you the true meaning of love. In that case, all you can do is try your best to love others in the hope that at some point they, too, will love you.

I was blessed in that I always knew I was loved and wanted by my family. From the very beginning, they showed me what love meant, and what it looked like when put into action.

Anna Mary Baldo, my mother, and her twin sister, Frances, were born on July 12, 1924, to my grandmother, who was just eighteen years old. She already had a two-year-old daughter, Carmella, who she nicknamed Millie.

My mother, gazing at me. I knew she loved me enormously. She got "sick" when I was around 6 years old. I always wanted to save her, and my Aunt Frances, too, but sadly, I couldn't.

She grew up in an area of Rochester still known as "Dutch Town" on Jay Street. The neighborhood consisted of immigrant families, including those who were Irish and Polish, although most of the population was Italian and German.

She often repeated the standard parent stories of her school days: she and her sisters trudged through Arctic temperatures over hill and dale, allegedly uphill both ways. The distances covered daily were immense before they reached their educational destination.

The walk home was just as unpleasant, only altered by the daily question my mother repeated over and over:

"What did I learn today? Tell me, what did I learn?"

Her two sisters would giggle, knowing they could say nothing that would satisfy her, and amused by my mom putting down her schooling. They never tired of the ritual that continued into their high school years.

School was not my mother's favorite, but she and Aunt Frances did enjoy business classes and were experts in typing class.

That all changed when a new boy named Joe caught her attention. He was neat and clean and had baby blue eyes like crystal jewels. The two of them immediately developed a friendship that continued to grow.

As twins do, my mom and Frances would play tricks on him. Since they often dressed alike, they were very successful.

My dad would say goodbye to my mother, and moments later she would appear in front of him in nearly impossible ways. My aunt would wink or do something funny, and he would become very confused.

It didn't take him long to catch on once he realized Anna had a twin, but they had a lot of fun in the meantime.

*High School yearbook photo of my mom and
and her identical twin sister, Frances. 1943.*

As their friendship deepened, the couple fell in love. My mother's family fell in love with my dad as well, who had been orphaned at thirteen. By age twenty, the two of them decided to get married.

This went against the wishes of my grandparents. It wasn't that they didn't like or even love my dad. But with World War II happening, they wanted my mother to wait until my dad was out of the service and home safely. They feared if he was shipped overseas, he might not return, or would return missing an arm or a leg. They also feared he might be so changed by the war that he would no longer be the same man she fell in love with. They were trying to spare her heartache.

But my mom was determined. There was no stopping her once her mind was made up. There were two decisions she always told me she was 100% sure were the right ones. The first was marrying my dad. The second was adopting me.

They married. The war ended, and my dad returned no worse for the wear. My grandparents forgave her and got over her denying them the chance to throw her a big wedding.

Just as other couples did, my parents struggled from time to time, too. They tried for a long time to have children. Seven years into their marriage, my mom had one child, but stillborn because she suffered from toxemia. Ten long years and a hysterectomy later, they adopted me.

The things that mattered to most people never really mattered to my mother. She never worried about having money or having things. She always knew, and told me too, that the things that mattered most were love and family, and you were rich if you had both of those.

Despite her dedication to gratitude, my mother was plagued with every conceivable illness throughout the years, some requiring surgeries. She suffered from intestinal problems, diabetes, and more. Depression, high blood pressure, and the resulting debilitating headaches drove her to prescription drug addiction. This meant that much of the time in my childhood when my dad was absent, I would be her caretaker and as a result often the target of her anger and frustration.

But despite those obstacles, she was still able to accomplish a lot, and her goal was to shape me into a decent human being.

By the time I was grown and had daughters of my own, she still struggled with her health, but always made time for them. Macular degeneration caused her to lose most of her eyesight toward the end of her life, and that broke her heart most of all, as she could barely see the granddaughters she cherished so much.

Her love, despite her issues, shaped me into the sensitive and caring person I am today. But above all, she taught me resilience.

Chapter Five: Resilience and "Angela"

Hardship was always a part of my mother's life, and therefore of mine. But what is the limit to hardship, and where is the point where it stops building character and instead destroys a person, causing them to feel so hopeless and bitter that they simply give up?

As I mentioned, my parents tried to get pregnant, and seven years after they were married, when my mom was twenty-six years old, they finally succeeded. She was destined to have a hard pregnancy.

First, early on, she was found unconscious on the floor of her apartment. Apparently, she hadn't smelled a gas leak coming from the stove, and had she not been found, she would have died.

That winter, her mother came down with pneumonia, and while caring for her, my very pregnant mother also caught it. This was exceptionally hard on her.

But the final incident in her pregnancy is a story I heard often. My parents got a cat because their apartment had mice and rats, and they wanted one to help control them.

One night, as my mother slept, she was awoken abruptly by the cat landing on her pregnant belly. She woke up screaming. My parents fully believed that because of that scare, my mom developed a complication known as toxemia or preeclampsia.

This condition causes high blood pressure in a pregnant woman, and while there is no direct proof, my parents believed the cat to be guilty. At eight months along, she became so ill she had to be hospitalized.

The doctors told her the baby had died, but that because she was so far along, she would have to carry the baby to term.

Whether this was because she had to have time to heal and get her blood pressure under control before she could deliver the baby, or for some other reason they could not perform surgery, she would have to complete her pregnancy.

After she delivered the baby, my parents named their daughter Angela after my grandmother Angelina.

That was January 31, 1952. My mother did not ever see her baby or hold her. She regretted not having a memorial for her. She never forgave herself for those things.

Ten years later, I became their daughter, but they made sure as I got older that I understood I was not a replacement daughter or some kind of consolation prize. In fact, they emphasized to me that it was God who wanted them to have me.

The stillbirth of my sister, who I would never meet in my lifetime, was just the start of her struggles. As I have said, my mother suffered from many illnesses.

Despite those struggles, she tried to teach me to be sensitive to others going through hard times. I felt an incredible connection to her even though we did not share the same biology, and because of her conditions, I learned that very lesson.

My mother often showed me horrific stories, I believe in an attempt to teach me to show compassion to others who were suffering. I remember distinctly her showing me a story in the newspaper about a child, living in Ireland, who was tarred and feathered by his parents. Why would she show me this story?

In fact, and likely because of examples like this, I became highly sensitive just like she was. I could tune into her moods, sense what she was feeling from her behavior patterns, and I don't know if that was a good or bad thing. Our gut connection helped me better deal with her even in the toughest of times.

I know now that what I experienced is explained as "clairsentience," a deep and unbreakable emotional attachment to someone; the ability to sense other people's emotions. Someone experiencing this can sense the past, present, or future physical and emotional states of others without using the standard five senses of smell, vision, touch, hearing, or taste. I became hypersensitive in this way to survive the chaos and volatility of my mother's unpredictable behavior. My mind told me I had to find patterns of predictability within the constant chaos. My survival depended upon this skill, and I learned to do it well. I felt I had to, or else. Living in this anticipatory state, of course, caused me to grow up with a lot of anxiety.

This attachment began at a very early age, shortly after my parents brought me home. They were soon to endure the things all parents do, including Night Feedings.

Chapter Six: Night Feedings

My parents had anticipated becoming parents for a long time, but no one is ever truly ready for their first child. For them, in October of 1962 when they brought me home, everything changed.

I was told stories over and over of the two of them jumping out of bed to rush to my side during the night, sometimes literally getting stuck in the door jamb and fighting over who would reach me first.

The obvious reason for my crying and waking was that I wanted to be fed. It was time for my night feeding.

Initially, I had a canopy crib, but later, as I grew, that turned into a canopy bed all my girlfriends from school envied.

As new parents, they did not know some of the things that other parents might find obvious. When I first started taking a bottle, my face would redden, and I would start to sweat. I would consume no more than an ounce or a little more of formula, and then I would fall asleep, exhausted. An hour later, I would wake up grumpy and hungry again.

My mother told me she finally discovered that the holes in the nipples of the bottle were too small, and I was starving, struggling to eat what I needed so desperately. But together, my mom and dad figured it out.

My dad was smaller in stature, at only five foot five, and so devoted was he, he decided it was a good idea to climb into my crib with me. He did so on some nights, eager to be close to me and comfort me as I slept.

Many years later, when I had my own daughter, my dad once again came to the rescue.

My family was in the habit of love bombing us, wanting to take care of the first grandchild, and make sure my husband Rick and I had time to ourselves.

One night, the entire bunch shooed us out of the house for some much-needed time together as a couple so they could watch our daughter, Shannon.

She started to cry, as infants do, but she seemed inconsolable. She kept crying no matter what they tried. My aunt, grandmother, and mother grew very nervous.

They went down the checklist of things to do. Diaper inspection: good and clean. They burped her. Nothing. They bounced her, rocked her, tried to play with her. Nothing.

She kept crying.

"What could possibly be wrong?" they said. Everyone was thinking the worst, but no one wanted to call me.

Prayer and seeking help from Jesus along with my grandmother's hand wringing and even the brief but sincere desire to call 9-1-1 surfaced as options.

But my dad, the five-foot five-man in the situation, gathered his courage to face them, grabbed a bottle of formula, and heated it to just the right temperature.

When it was ready, he walked calmly to my daughter and popped it in her mouth. She started to eat and stopped crying.

The cries of alarm, the hand wringing, the fervent praying all stopped. The women stared, hushed, and in awe of my father.

The Baby Whisperer.

He shook his head. "What the hell is wrong with all of you?" he asked. "The kid was just hungry."

My dad was always the voice of reason. This incident was just one small example of his brilliance.

Chapter Seven: Hallmark Cards and Hell

As I grew, the night feedings and stuff of infancy stopped, and my mother expected more of me.

She slammed her fists on the kitchen table and screamed:

"That's not right, God damnit!"

I cowered. I was five, and trying, really trying to do what she asked, and do it the right way.

"You messed this up!"

"These cards are so expensive! Erase it, fix it!" she howled at me.

I wanted to cry. It was summertime, the kitchen was warm, and my small, sweaty arms stuck to the plastic tablecloth and made a funny sound every time I pulled them free.

I felt scared and ashamed, but her hollering continued. She flew into a rage. This was not the first time I'd seen her like this, and unfortunately, it would not be the last.

I'd obviously committed some offense. Her instructions for me were simple: write out greeting cards to family members for whatever occasion was at hand. Her impossibly high standards for perfection were outside of my young abilities. Combined with her lack of patience, this created an impossible situation for me.

I knew there was something wrong and different about my mother, even then. Still, I couldn't understand her incredible level of rage.

I mean, I knew what I had apparently done so wrong. My pen had smeared on a word or two, and I tried to erase it, to please her.

"That is so messy!" she yelled as I tried to erase ink from the paper. She continued her rant.

"Don't you realize how expensive those cards are? Do you even care?"

She pounded her fists some more.

I remained silent.

I was left-handed, and so often my pinky finger would drag across the writing and smear if I did not wait for it to dry. Still, I tried to write perfectly what she wanted.

But I couldn't. My five-year-old attempts didn't measure up.

Effort didn't matter. What I did was not correct. It was not perfect. She screamed the words and let me know.

These card-writing "sessions" happened often throughout my childhood and I always dreaded them. I still remember them clearly, fifty years later.

Sometimes in these sessions, she became so angry she would rip the card from my tiny grasp, tear it to shreds, and toss the pieces dramatically into the air.

"You've done it now!" she would shout.

There was no way I could make it right.

Every time she called me to the kitchen, and I saw the cards spread out there, my heart dropped. I knew what would follow: disapproval and rage.

The card writing slowed as I grew older, and her rage faded as I was able to write better and I understood I better do it perfectly, or else.

So, I tried. Tried hard.

But this was only one manifestation of my mom's problems. You see, as much as she loved me, her struggles with depression and mental illness, perhaps much of it due to the small child she had to carry to stillbirth and her ongoing battle with depression led to worse things than Hallmark card sessions.

Sometimes much worse. She would lie in her bed for two to three days, her speech incoherent, her face contorted, looking two or three decades beyond her years.

She stayed in pajamas, never getting dressed. I would hide away in my room, scared, praying, and wondering what was going on. Sometimes she would call out, screaming obscenities, insults, and the vilest things you could imagine about me. Years later I look back and think about all the verbal abuse she heaped upon me, in this altered state, and still do not know how I survived it, and the effects and toll it took on me not only as a child, but as an adult.

I later learned it was the pills, the medication she was on that set her off into these episodes.

The rants would last sometimes for minutes, hours, or even days. I learned to breathe between them, taking comfort in the silence until they started up again. Any little rustle, a sound from my room, any evidence that I was present could set her off. I prayed she would sleep it off.

My dad worked both day and night to support us. I often had to fend for myself when this was happening. When she was this bad, sometimes he would stop between jobs to feed me something, otherwise, I would be on my own.

When things got too scary, which they often did, I felt like she could be dangerous or even threatening. I would phone my dad at work or try to secretly phone my aunt, staying as quiet as possible so my mother would not hear.

Sometimes, my aunt would come rescue me. Others, my father would come home from work and try to load my mom's body, either dead weight or a struggling mass, into the car to take her to the hospital.

I never was told, nor did I ask, what happened to her there or how a hospital would help her.

I did know my father was afraid during those times that she might overdose and die.

That scared me, too. My mother, the mother fate had chosen for me, was sick and addicted, and I didn't understand why.

Those were the hell times, and I often felt hatred for her then rather than pity. I was too young to care about anyone but myself or to actually take care of myself. I wanted to understand why she was making me, my dad, and our family suffer like this.

Many times, I would go to my aunt's house and stay there, sometimes for days or even weeks. I feared going home, but eventually, my parents would force me to do so. I would be sworn to secrecy. I could never reveal what happened with my mother at home.

When she came to her senses, she would apologize and tell me she loved me.

"It won't ever happen again," she would promise.

Even from a young age, I knew what she said was a lie, and I hated her in those moments for her empty promises.

She loved me. I mostly loved her, but sometimes resented her and felt like I hated her. I felt guilty about that. Even as a child I knew it wasn't right to "hate" your own mom, and I was angry about being put in that position. I often asked myself, "why me?"

Rinse, wash, repeat. Like the directions on a shampoo bottle, the cycle just continued over and over. Fear. Verbal abuse. Addiction. They all ruled her life. Our lives.

By age eight or nine I was an expert at telling my mother's weather. I could identify her volatility, her patterns of behavior, and knew when to expect her to be unpredictable.

She tried to pin her descent back into addiction on something we did: punishment or retribution or the result of something someone in the family did: her sisters, her husband, or even me.

I knew this to be complete and total bullshit. Even then, I refused to accept any blame for her behavior and realized early on that it had nothing to do with me or anyone else. Her actions belonged to her and her alone.

While I didn't recognize her verbal abuse by that name, I knew with everything else I had to put up with from her, I didn't need to add blame to the equation. I often expressed the same to my dad, aunts, and grandmother.

Despite knowing her issues, and recognizing they were not my fault, I still tried to be the "perfect child" in hopes that it might help her in some way. That was never enough to stop the downward spiral and the continued episodes of abuse.

She continued to try to numb whatever internal hell she was enduring to silence the pain with copious amounts of Darvon, Percocet, and other drugs.

No matter what she ingested, or how much, she could not seem to quiet or kill the demons and the pain inside.

To my great disappointment I learned, and, of course, I say this sarcastically:

At least she wasn't a quitter.

I know I have shared how lucky I was to have my family, to be adopted by the parents I was, and it's true. There were good times between the crazy times. In fact, my mom was great between the crazy times.

Chapter Eight: Between the Crazy Times

When my mother was well, life was grand. When she wasn't, it was hell.

Despite her issues, I was always confident she loved me more than life itself. I could see even early on that she had no idea how to crawl out of the mess she was in. And while my family sometimes talked about my mother's addiction, they were all at a loss as to what to do to help her.

None of them had much education and they did not know the options open to them, if there were any, and their collective helplessness did not give me hope. I wasn't necessarily stoic behind closed doors, but I was basically told to never discuss my mother's issues or problems with anyone outside the family, especially with anyone at school. Not knowing any better, or how to seek outside help on my own, I obeyed.

Although addiction is made up of highs and lows, I secretly feared she enjoyed the highs too much to be able to stop her behavior. She seemingly did anything she could to continue getting them even if the crash left her sick as a dog. Even knowing this was part of her addiction, to say it made me angry is an understatement. I felt rage at her behavior.

As I have said, my parents often told me I was chosen. I suppose knowing this made me feel special in one way, but then as my mother's illness grew worse, I wondered why I had been chosen to have her rather than a more "normal" mother.

My mother also carried a lot of guilt, this I know. She and I had a roller-coaster relationship. She would be abusive with her words when she was under the influence of drugs. When she got clean and off the pills, she would come pleading to me during her "make-up" phase to forgive her.

Any recovery, even short lived, was always due to my dad or my family trying to get her help. I told them that I hated her every time I was taken from my house and went to live with my Aunt Millie.

Then, of course, I felt guilty. My dad would force me to go back home even though I did not want to. Though I was angry and bitter, I was forced to forgive her. She always promised, as addicts do, that the bad behavior would not happen again, but I knew in my heart it would.

Time after time, she proved me right. It was a vicious cycle and always ended in disappointment and heartbreak. She lied to me over and over, teaching me I could never completely trust her.

Despite all our conflicts, I felt very connected to her. I could sense her emotions and could feel when she was about to go on another of her pill rampages.

My mother, who got her hair done at the neighborhood hairdresser every Friday, had a phobia about her hair and her appearance. Some of her meanest and nastiest times came when her hair was all done up and she looked her best. Those were the times she treated me horribly. Did I imagine this? Was there some connection to her getting her hair done and then railing at me even more? I can remember knockdown, drag-out fights between my parents over my mother's hair!

Silly as this must sound, this was part of her mental illness. If we went out anywhere on those fateful Fridays, I knew I was in for it.

However, when her hair was not done, she skipped many family outings, parties, and weddings, all because she was petrified that she didn't look presentable enough. She would often send my father to these events alone.

Also, she stressed constantly about her speech, and how she sounded or spoke when talking with others on the phone or in person. These fears got so bad she almost developed a stutter when speaking on the phone.

Sometimes I felt my existence was for the sole purpose of fulfilling her need to be a mother, but then why was she being so terrible to me?

Despite her awful moments, my mother was a complex, contradictory, and very resilient person. Even though often lost in her addiction, she was indestructible and there was no arguing with her, ever.

While she could not seem to get herself together during ordinary times, whenever a family crisis arose, she was the first one to rise to the occasion. In fact, she seemed to thrive on being needed during those times. When my grandfather was sick shortly after a stroke (and after several previous heart attacks) my mom rushed to his side and took care of him. She supported and comforted my grandmother.

Many years later, when my dad almost died from a heart attack and bypass surgery that followed, it was my mom who nursed him back to health.

One of my worst memories was at about age 9 or 10, when my Aunt Millie invited me to go to lunch with her, my grandmother, and a couple of her "lady friends" at a chain restaurant called Charlie Bubbles. It was sort of a precursor to a TGIF Fridays.

These ladies loved going out and trying new places, and my mother had been invited to come along this time, but she was in one of her worst "episodes."

She was home in her pajamas even though it was daytime on a sunny, summer afternoon, and had taken quite a few pills by lunchtime. Her hair was plastered to her head, she looked at least 20 years older than her age.

She'd already been mean and angry to me, and I was afraid of her and what might come next. I was relieved when my aunt called me and said she was picking me up. I told my mother I was going to lunch with my aunt.

My mother was in her bed at this point, and I don't remember if she started cussing at me or not, but I just grabbed a sweater and went outside to wait.

The restaurant was nice. Everything was accented with brass, from the railings to the handles on the restroom doors, and colorful balloon bouquets floated next to each booth. it was just a fun, cheerful place.

Because I was worried and upset about my mom, even a happy event like this was marred for me. Even at that young age, I could not get my mind off my mother at home to fully enjoy it. I knew what awaited me there.

My grandmother smiled but eyed me nervously during the meal and I could see the love, affection, and worry painted all over her sweet face. It made me both sad and embarrassed. I felt guilty, almost as if my mother's issues were my fault, a heavy cross to bear as a child.

Eventually, our lunch ended but I could not have predicted what would happen next. My Aunt drove me home and dropped me off. I went into the breezeway that led into the garage. When I tried the kitchen door it was locked. I knocked. Nothing. I banged on the door. Nothing. I yelled for my mother. Nothing. Now I walked out front. At that time, there were no cell phones, nor was there a simple way to call someone from outside the house.

Granted it was a warm summer day, but my aunt was gone already, I was alone, and my dad was at work. One of my aunts lived about a mile or so away, and I could have walked. My mother's twin lived across the street, but I don't remember if she wasn't home or what other reason I might not have wanted to go over there. My grandmother lived just up the street, but I didn't want to go there and upset her. I considered walking over to my Aunt Millie's house, but I had to cross a busy highway to get there, and I was forbidden to cross that road.

Finally, my mother literally stumbled to the door and opened it. I went inside, very afraid.

She hollered and cursed at me as if I had committed some terrible crime:

"Oh, you went to lunch with your Aunt Millie, did you?"

"Did you have a GOOD TIME?" she screeched, though her speech was slurred, and she could barely stand.

"You are just all about YOUR GOOD TIME, aren't you? Aren't you?"

"You don't care if your mother is home, alone or sick, do you? DO YOU?"

The line of questioning went on and on.

I went into my bedroom and shut my door. Within a few minutes, I called my aunt secretly to tell her I had been locked out of the house and my mother was acting irrationally and subjecting me to her anger and abuse.

"I'll be right there," she said, as she had many times before.

I must give myself some credit, too, for learning coping mechanisms to deal with my mother's illness.

Despite my loneliness and sadness, I tried to focus on school and be the best student I could possibly be.

I felt the urgent need to do everything to be "perfect" to make my parents proud because I realized that they sacrificed a lot for me in buying me beautiful things, sending me to private, Catholic schools, and trying to make me happy despite what was happening with my mother. I knew their stories of hardship and poverty growing up, how little they had, and yet they wanted to give me everything and make me happy.

Teachers told my parents I was creative, or rather imaginative. I think I used daydreaming and going off into my own fantasy world as a means of survival. As a child, my friends and I entertained ourselves for hours making up stories, role-playing, and making our own fun, acting out little skits and plays in my bedroom and our backyard. We were the writers and directors of our own stories.

This is how we entertained ourselves. Words saved me because I was constantly fantasizing, writing stories in my own head, reading books, listening to music, and really thinking about the songs, the lyrics, and their meanings, and dreaming of happier times.

Long lonely periods in my bedroom spent reading and listening to music helped me drown out my mother's verbal abuse that sometimes went on for hours at a time. I learned to be a survivor. People have teased me for not paying attention, for "zoning out" at times, but I think I just taught myself to "go somewhere else" mentally when I was overwhelmed. That was the one thing I could control even if I could not get away from my mother at her worst. I learned no one could control my thoughts or feelings, that I had ultimate power over those. That was a relief and a blessing.

Baking and cooking with my grandmother were also wonderful. I think she tried to keep me occupied and make me forget about the horrors of my mother's behavior, but also because she loved those things. She felt teaching me would not only distract me from my mother's bad behavior, but it was also a way to bond with me and teach me some Italian traditions and cooking skills.

My mother's illness caused me to suffer lifelong anxiety. My brain goes a mile a minute and I am always afraid I will "miss" something. I was always on alert, always listening for the time my dad would get home from bartending so I could safely allow myself to relax and fall asleep. To this day, I have severe insomnia, and I am sure it dates to my childhood. I am proud of the fact that not only have I learned to live with it, but I am triumphing over it.

I marvel now in retrospect at the bipolar existence I experienced because of living with a very sick mother. I also marvel at how so much was still accomplished in my family. So many happy times, so much life was lived and experienced, by me and them as well. They managed, somehow to produce large blocks of normalcy for me between the crazy times, and their resilience was something to behold through all the struggles they faced.

But struggle was nothing new for my dad. Things were hard for him from the time he was young, and hardship was his constant companion.

Chapter Nine: The Final Curtain

The grandmother I never met, Marietta, lay in a pool of her own blood. She was 37, and dead from a self-inflicted abortion.

Her death left my 4-year-old dad, Joseph, and his three brothers, Bart, Phillip, and Albert, and three sisters, Rose, Anna, and Pearl, without a mother, and her husband, Vincenzo, without a wife. She had seven mouths to feed, plus herself and her husband. She found herself pregnant again, devoid of modern medical options, and unable to afford them even if they were available. It was 1929, the height of the Great Depression.

As a child, I often heard stories of her passing, but it was years before I learned the true cause of her death. My dad spoke of how funerals happened then, a wake with calling hours held in people's homes.

My dad Joseph and his brothers, with their father, Vincenzo DiProspero, center. Left to right: Dad's oldest brother Bardo, my dad, and Uncles Albert and Phillip. Circa 1932.

My dad's memories were quite vivid for a four-year-old boy. He recalled death, sadness, fear. A coffin sat in their living room and a notice declaring the wake of his mother, Marietta DiProspero, hung over the front door.

One of the few pictures of my dad as a little boy. Photo shows a date of 1929, which would make Dad 4 years old. That was the year his mother died.

My father was fluent in Italian, his first language, until his mother's death. But since his dad wanted all the children to be successful in school and to acclimate, they didn't speak it much at home after she died, focusing instead on English. The loss of the ability to speak his native language equated to the loss of the essence of his mother. After her death, things went black for him, both literally and figuratively.

His memories became mere glimpses into a childhood filled with events, none of them good or happy times. The four boys slept in a single bed. The family had no help.

Bath water was only clean for the first child who used it. All the others followed, none wanting to be the unfortunate last one, bathing in tepid and grimy water. He tried to be first whenever possible.

Meals consisted of bread and black coffee, supplemented with pasta on occasion. My father spoke of the infrequent treat of Italian polenta, a cornmeal paste that would be mixed on a large cutting board and shaped into a rectangular form. Each child would then pull some toward them, splitting it as equally as they could, and then consuming it.

The brothers were all small, my dad perhaps the smallest. He was a fussy eater despite his hunger, and from time to time my grandfather would take pity on him since he was such a sweet child. He would buy some shaved Virginia ham and give him a small amount.

On Christmas Eve, they would hang up Christmas stockings in a living room devoid of a tree or any other decorations. But they knew if they hung those stockings, some kind of magic would happen, and

Santa Claus would stop at their humble home and leave them gifts.

He spoke of the magic of those Christmas mornings when they would wake to find an orange and a few walnuts, still in the shells, in their stockings. What a treat in such times of poverty!

Their father, though poor, worked diligently to give his children these moments of wonder.

Food had a high value to him and those of his generation who survived the Great Depression. Even years later, if anyone ordered dessert when we were out, my dad would marvel if any of it remained uneaten. He declared how this would never have happened when he was a boy.

My dad's family also happened to have a history of severe heart disease in nearly all the male members. My dad, his brothers, and later, his nephews all struggled with it.

In the winter of 1938 in upstate New York, after a particularly appealing snowfall, my dad and his brothers decided to go out at dusk to go sledding.

Of course, their "sleds" were made of large pieces of found cardboard, their coats, and pants shabby and worn.

They had a great time, boys being boys, rolling around in the snow-covered grass, sliding down what hills they could find.

By the time they went back in the house, cold and wet, snow-packed all over their meager clothes, their father had arrived home from work.

He took one look at them and lost his temper. He screamed at them about ruining the few clothes they had, getting sick from being outside in the elements.

In typical ranting parent fashion, he ordered everyone to bed. He was clearly stressed, agitated, and overwhelmed. He hollered as he herded his children into their rooms, and exhausted from a hard day of work, went to bed himself.

He never woke up.

The next morning, the boys went to find him in his room, to apologize for their clearly terrible and callous behavior, at least, in their young perception.

They never got the chance. Their father was dead of an apparent heart attack.

My dad, young Joseph, only 13, went from being a motherless child to being an orphan in one tragic night. He had to explain to his baby brother, Al, that they would never see their father walking home from work ever again.

He wasn't coming back.

And my dad would spend most of his life secretly and silently blaming himself for his father's death. He regretted that he never got to say, "Dad, I'm sorry," or "Dad, I love you."

Throughout his life, he would visit his parents' graves at the cemetery. When I was young, he often took me with him. I hope that he imagined his father saying to him: "It's okay, son. It wasn't your fault." I believe most parents would have said the same in this scenario.

And I hope he came to believe the words he could only imagine hearing.

As to this young boy, my father's future, he would find he could only rely on one person: himself.

Chapter Ten: Blistered Fingers and New Parents

At the age of 13, and now an orphan, Joseph pulled on his clothes each morning. He learned quickly how to fend for himself. His clothes were worn and wrinkled, but clean. He ran a comb through his jet-black hair, which fell in a wave over the top of his head. A muscular boy, he wore a plain but relaxed short-sleeve shirt, pleated trousers, and penny loafers. He looked like a movie star, but he didn't think such things of himself.

He grabbed his books, a piece of stale bread, and threw on his shabby winter coat before heading out the door. There was no one to say goodbye to, no one to wish him a good day at school. His mother was long deceased, his father recently so, and his sister worked long hours to support the newly orphaned family. She was gone long before he headed out the door.

All he knew was self-reliance, the only thing that sustained him now.

He didn't give much thought to what he had or didn't have, he just put one foot in front of the other and kept going.

Survival was all that mattered. He walked to school, alone every day. Even before my dad's father died, at only 9 or 10 years old he was working in fields not far from home in the summer, picking crops for something like a dollar a week. He slept on a hard, salt cot and worked from dawn until dusk picking beans for pennies per basket.

But he needed the job to help his father support a starving family. Many stories of his childhood were things I didn't learn until I was in my 30s. My dad didn't want to complain or to tell me tales that might make me feel sad or sorry for him.

Once I learned how difficult his childhood must have been, I had even more respect for him than ever before.

Shortly after his father died, a miracle happened, something I believe helped save him.

He met a girl named Anna Baldo, who would eventually become his wife. Anna's family was relatively well off. The pair met in school, where Anna and her twin sister would often play tricks on Joseph. Anna would turn up here and there and he would be beside himself wondering how she could be in different places so quickly or in other situations that seemed impossible unless Anna had a body double.

Joseph quickly found out she did, indeed, have a body double, and that "double" would turn out to be an identical twin, sister, Frances. While Anna's sister was good-natured in her acceptance of Joseph, her father was not a fan of boys dating his daughters.

My Grandfather, Tony Baldo, although a man with a great sense of humor and a good businessman, also had a temper. He never hit my grandmother, but she did often fear his moods and reactions to things.

My beloved maternal grandparents, Anthony (Tony) and Angelina (Salvaggio) Baldo, in the 1970s.

The girls were not allowed to date, not at 13, and boys were not allowed in the house. I would learn later why my grandfather, who owned a bar, felt this way so strongly.

The family had a large player piano, and one day my father and the man who would later become my

Aunt Millie's husband, my Uncle Tom, were at the house while my mom's father was at work.

A fight had broken out at his bar, as they sometimes did, and he had blood on his shirt, so he ran home to change. My grandmother hid the boys behind that player piano while he was there, fearful of what he would do if he found them in the house.

My Grandmother Angelina took pity on my dad, who at the time was this young, parentless boy, and fed him often. He'd found love in this new family and my mother, Anna. He thought about her all the time.

But he still had to work. His sister needed his help in making money so the family could survive. Since he was a senior in high school by this time and already had enough credits to graduate, he would leave school at noon every day, sometimes before.

He would head to Clapp's Baby Food, which was a precursor to Gerber baby food and one of the first, if not the first, baby food companies in the country. It was located in my hometown in the City of Rochester, New York. My dad performed several different tasks as part of his work there.

This is an advertisement for Clapp's baby food, located at 460 Buffalo Road in Rochester, NY, and was the precursor to the Gerber baby food factory. Clapp's was the first company to manufacture and sell jarred baby food in the U.S. Working conditions in the early 1940s were like the sweatshops of long ago. This is where my dad worked while finishing up his senior year of high school, at Madison High School in Rochester, NY, before enlisting in the United States Army Air Corps. (USAAF).

Jars of hot, cooked baby food, freshly canned, would come down a conveyor belt by the hundreds in several different lines.

Workers perched over these fast-moving belts, ready to grab the jars, still boiling hot, and toss them into large cooling tubs. They would often blister their hands as they did so.

Joseph knew the drill well. After many blisters, he decided to wear gloves to protect his fingers. But the gloves didn't work well, and the jars often slipped out of his grip. So, he cut the fingertips off so he could better grasp the jars. The belt didn't stop, and he had to keep up.

Without fingertips, the gloves did little good. His hands were always red, blistered, and painful. This was his job, though, and he needed the money.

But Joseph also had another task. Small in stature, he was also strong. He would be lowered into the large concrete mixers next to the giant mixing blade. The sides were coated with the residue of dried baby food.

The interior of the mixer was hot, and Joseph had to wear a loose uniform over his body. He would scrub the walls of the mixers daily, a claustrophobic hell.

Working next to the giant blades, he often thought those in the control room above would forget he was inside and turn the mixers on. He imagined being ground up along with the baby food, and the fear of this happening never lessened no matter how often he performed this task.

Despite his fears, he never asked questions about what security measures might be in place to avoid this imagined scenario, if any. He just went to work, did his job, day after day, grateful for the extra 35 cents a day.

One afternoon, it began raining after he left school. When he got out of work, very late, it was still raining, only harder. He walked home, tired, and hungry. He arrived at home, what was by then his sister's house, to find her husband, who was a nasty alcoholic, quite angry with him for his tardiness.

The door was locked. He knocked and called out, but no one answered. His sister's husband had decided this would be his punishment.

My father spent the night in the pouring rain, freezing, cold, hungry, and tired, until morning when he was allowed inside.

"That will teach you never to be late again," his sister's husband said.

My dad stayed through high school. He worked hard. His love for my mother grew, and despite the many obstacles he faced, he graduated and then enlisted in the Army.

My dad, Joseph. Military photo. He was so handsome, with those "baby blues."

He was young and healthy and in love.

Maybe we can have a good life together, he thought to himself.

He and his beautiful, waif-like, sweet Anna.

Small in stature, but muscular, with blistered fingers from his hard work: that was my beautiful father, who's life would soon change forever.

*My parents, Joseph and Anna, standing up
for a wedding around 1946.*

Chapter Eleven: The Three Sisters

My grandmother, Angelina, wore her winter coat in the middle of summer. She was eighteen years old, pregnant with twins, and she'd gained about 70 pounds.

She'd given birth two years before, to a little girl she named Carmella, but my grandfather later nicknamed her Millie and that is the name that stuck. She was my mom's oldest sister, my aunt.

In those days, they gave women ether to render them unconscious for the birth, and children were often born at home, which was the case with my mother and her twin sister, Frances. I don't know how soon after the doctor arrived that the ether was administered. What I do know is that the twins were born breech and weighed over seven pounds each.

My grandparents, Angelina (Salvaggio) and Anthony Baldo, on their wedding day, September 16, 1920. She was 14 (turned 15 about three weeks later) and he was 27. Marrying young was common in those days, I was told. My grandfather actually had his eye on my grandmother's older sister, Frances, but she was not interested. My grandmother told her parents that she "liked" my grandfather, and her family arranged a wedding date! The rest is history.

The twins. Aunt Frances, left, and my mother Anna, right. Taken around 1930, when they were about 5 years old.

They were named Anna Mary and Frances Mary.

Just barely an adult, my grandmother found herself with three children, a husband who worked long hours at his business, a bar. There were no washers or dryers, no disposable diapers or many other conveniences mothers today take for granted.

I heard that, at one time, she was forced to make her own diapers out of cloth sugar bags, which she boiled to get the logo off and sterilize the cloth, and then sewed parts of them together.

Their absorbency was, well, questionable at best. A type of rubber pants was often worn over these insufficient cloth diapers to prevent them from leaking.

Life was hard to stay the least.

Breastfeeding was the norm in those days. And there were meals to be made and a thousand other chores to be done.

Some relief came when my grandfather, who took pity on my grandmother, brought home one of the first automatic washers and dryers in the neighborhood.

The twins were often sickly, and my grandmother told me that at eighteen months, both developed walking pneumonia. My mom was admitted to the hospital, her sister Frances missed her, and began to "fail to thrive" as my grandmother put it. She refused to eat and didn't sleep well.

This incident showed just how bonded the twins were. When my mother returned home, Frances's entire demeanor changed.

Like other twins, they also developed their own way of communication. To hear my grandmother tell it, they often spoke in words no one else could understand when they talked to one another.

"It sounded like, 'Ollie, Ollie!'" my grandmother told me. "Whether that was just their way of calling to one another or the word meant something more, I could never tell."

This started before they were really talking when they were only eleven months old. This bond remained strong for their entire lives. They seemed to operate in tandem in various areas, including their physical and mental health, although that was often an odd balance.

If my mom was well, Frances was sick. If Frances was sick, mom was well. It was as if they were two halves of the same person, never able to fully function independently.

My grandmother, despite her lack of education, felt the twins didn't get the benefit of a "full egg" but only half of one. She felt this was the reason they were so sickly and "weaker."

Weaker than whom? Why, their older sister, Millie, of course, who in contrast to her sisters, was healthy from day one and remained so for her entire life. Because she was healthy and "good," she got less attention than her adorable and needy younger sisters.

The three sisters, my mom Anna, left, Aunt Millie,
center, and Aunt Frances, right.

Though older, she lived in their shadow, and when
my grandmother spoke to her, she often made fun of
her looks, in jest, of course.

My aunt went along with it and even made fun of herself as she got older. My grandmother would tell her that at birth, because of her darker skin, eyes, and the peach fuzzy lanugo babies are born with, "You looked like a monkey."

My Aunt Millie would laugh, and just say, "That's just the way I am."

Apart from making fun of her looks, my Aunt Millie was very close to my grandmother and described her as her best friend. She took after my grandfather's side of the family: educated and upscale.

My mom and her twin Frances often took after my grandmother's family, known to be alcoholics and those with a "reputation" in the worst context, not wanting to work that hard, and even lazy.

Millie did not possess the beauty of her twin sisters, but she was healthy, petite, and always easygoing. She was known for her sweetness and her sunny disposition. Though they often overshadowed her in some ways, the twins considered her to be the favored daughter.

The crankiness and illness of the twins could have been seen as a "foreshadowing" of the physical and mental illness that would dominate both of their lives.

Despite how different the three of them were, they were always the best of friends and nearly inseparable. The twins had a unique bond, certainly, but both looked up to their older sister.

In truth, their constant dark moods, chronic illness, and later depression and addiction to prescription meds wore on my aunt and her pleasantness. It led to some detachment and an emotionless type of blankness regarding their suffering at times.

She was as frustrated, or more so than the rest of us. Heartbroken, her patience tested and surpassed, and her understanding at her limit, she would often say about her sisters, "God helps those who help themselves."

We all, at one point or another, reached the point where we didn't know what to do anymore to help them face their problems.

Truthfully, my aunt had a heart that was ten times the size of her 95-pound stature. When life was hard due to my mother's illness, she was often my lifeline. She became a mother to all her nieces and nephews, but she especially became a second mother to me.

Later she would serve as a grandmother to my children, especially after my mom's death. We will get to that part of my story later.

My mother envied the relationship I had with my aunt.

"Aunt Millie is your favorite," she would say. "You love her more than you love me."

Truth be told, although I wouldn't or couldn't admit those things to myself, it was true. I loved them both, but differently, and always within my heart was the realization that I had but one mother, sick and flawed as she might have been, she was mine. My Aunt Millie was "like a mother," sometimes "another mother."

From a young age, I felt a deep debt of gratitude and loyalty to my parents for adopting me, but my aunt really did help me when things were bad.

I put a lot of pressure on myself. As my parents' only child, I also felt I was their "only shot" in life, so I pushed myself to be good, hold up my family name, and make them proud.

Despite the horrors my mom put me through due to her addiction, I loved her beyond anything she ever did. She and my father were all I knew. I tried desperately to mirror their love.

My aunt, though. She was a rule breaker. She marched to her own drummer, and she was shrewd, wise, and quirky. She and my Uncle Tom never had children, but she dedicated herself to her nieces and nephews instead. She cooked and sewed for the whole family and made sure we were well dressed.

She did all this on her antique sewing machine with a trundle foot she had to pump. Her "spare bedroom" which was more of a sewing room, was filled with little canisters containing sewing paraphernalia. Among them sat an old-fashioned pin cushion, the one that looked like a tomato, filled with colorful pins. The drawers in that room were stuffed with all kinds of colorful fabric and scraps.

Alterations were her strong suit rather than creating something from scratch, and she was always inventing new ways to mend something or enhance it. For years, she would iron my husband's and daughters' work clothes and dresses with precision.

She learned all this at a dress shop in the city where she worked for over forty years.

My aunts were only part of the support system that I depended on. But really, everything started when my mother made the decision to marry my father.

Chapter Twelve: Walla Walla Wedding

During his time in the Army, my dad wrote constant love letters to my mom, stating his love for her and how much he missed her. Like many couples at the time, they had a typical 1940s "Notebook-movie-worthy" love affair. They were separated by the war, and eagerly awaited marriage and a "normal" life.

When my dad returned to the states in 1945, my mom packed her bags without telling her parents, and, in April, headed for Walla Walla, Washington, to what is now the Walla Walla Regional Airport. However, in 1945, was a U.S. Army Air Force base.

Much to the dismay of her older sister, Millie, who told her that her plans for eloping would "kill Daddy," and in the company of her future sister-in-law, Mary, in late April she boarded a train.

The two women rode that train for five days, and only a few days after arriving, my parents were married by the Army chaplain. My mother was just 20 years old and wore a beautiful, traditional, long, white wedding gown and a white veil that accentuated her tiny figure. She carried a beautiful bouquet of white lilies. My dad's "Goombati," his best army friend, was their best man, and my mom's future sister-in-law, Mary, was her only attendant and maid of honor.

My parents' wedding photo, May 7, 1945, Armistice Day, Walla Walla, Washington. Left to right: Dad's best man, Anthony Cipiti, my dad Joseph, my mother Anna, and my aunt Mary DiProspero (Dad's brother Bart's wife). Mom eloped, taking a five-day train ride with my aunt to marry my father, the love of her life!

One of my biggest regrets is my loss of memory. Perhaps, I should have written the details I'd been told about these events sooner, things like the name of his best man. It is hard when your family members are all dead, and you are an only child and the "family historian" and you look around and remember that although you don't recall some of the details, there is no one left to ask for clarification.

I see my dad in my mind at times, shouting emphatically from heaven, "Yes, Diane, it was Walter!" or whatever the name he is trying to convey, whatever detail I am trying to remember.

I know he is trying to communicate this and more to me, to guide my memory the way he guided me in life. He protected me always, shared his knowledge, and was there for me.

He made sure I heard the stories often so I would remember them well.

There is a story about a time in Florida at the home of his in-laws. The men golfed and played bocce ball or other games, but not my father. He sat next to my bassinette, his newly adopted and precious baby girl, all day. The other men teased him for not leaving my side, but he couldn't care less what they said.

And now, writing his story, I feel him watching me. I feel him imploring me to get the names right, to remember the details he told me. I believe he knows I am writing this for him, for both of my parents and my entire family, to preserve their story and share their love story.

I'm doing my best. That makes me happy. Even death does not separate us now because the bond we shared was the deepest connection I have ever had with anyone. Dad fills my soul with his ever-present love and presence.

Joseph and Anna were married on May 7, 1945. Armistice Day.

Will my story be enough to express my eternal gratitude for what they sacrificed, and all they did for me through the years? I can only hope so, but knowing Dad, I believe he's looking down and his heart is full now, too.

Part Two

The two most important days in your life

are the day you are born

and the day you find out why.

— Mark Twain

Chapter Thirteen: The Jefferson Grill and National News

My grandfather, Anthony Baldo, immigrated from Italy to the United States, like many others, with the sole intent of becoming a successful businessman. Everyone called him Tony. He arrived when he was 22, sometime around 1916. Despite lacking formal education, he had a great head for business and investments. He married my grandmother five years later in 1920 or 1921, I am not quite sure the exact year, when he was 27 and she was only 15, some reports had her as young as 13 or 14.

My grandfather knew how to invest and stretch a penny. Although he could be strict with my grandmother and insisted on a weekly allowance that she had to adhere to for many years, he could be randomly generous as well. Although he could afford new things for my mother and her sisters, he almost always bought things second-hand. Sometimes, I recall my mother feeling sad when she was older, recalling that she once even had a bicycle that fell apart as she was riding it, causing her to hurt herself.

She knew instinctively, even as a child that her dad could have bought her a new bike but didn't, and although she wasn't ungrateful, the fact still stung.

Even though he had built a good portfolio of investments, he lost it all in the Great Depression.

When he first arrived in the United States, he worked as a butcher, and during Prohibition, he worked as a bootlegger. My grandmother often told me that he would strut down the street dressed in a suit and carrying a briefcase. People would mistake him for a doctor, but the briefcase was actually full of liquor, a different kind of medicine, I suppose.

The irony was that when he did go to the doctor, he would dress poorly, almost like a bum. He didn't want the doctor to know he had money, hoping he would get charged less for his appointments and prescriptions.

Sometime after the repeal of Prohibition, in the mid to late 1930s, he purchased a small building and opened his first bar on Jefferson Avenue in Rochester. By 1938, when many were struggling to emerge from the Great Depression, my grandfather was doing pretty well for himself.

Uncle Tom Maggio, left, and Dad, right. Dad was always known as "Little Joe". Here they are at Grandpa Baldo's bar, which later became theirs, "The Jefferson Grill," on Jefferson Avenue in Rochester, NY, also later the epicenter of the infamous 1964 race riots. They were always so happy at their place, doing what they loved best: serving their loyal patrons, schmoozing with them, and telling their jokes.

The backroom had a kitchen, and so they served food in addition to liquor. There were floor shows, risqué dancing girls at night and on the weekend. Because my grandfather was in the "bar business" and saw a lot of what he termed to be "loose women," he became extra strict with his own daughters. They were not allowed to go to the bar, and he was especially strict with my mom and aunts about boys and dating. When my parents met and fell in love, they were very young, and my grandfather's strict ways, common in those days, but even worse due to what he witnessed in his bar, made it especially hard for my mom and dad to have any kind of normal dating relationship.

I remember a long wooden bar and the old jukebox in the corner. On occasion, my dad would set me on top of the bar. I recall one instance when I was about four and looked at a customer sitting at the bar, and quipped, "Where's your wife?" to the thunderous laughs of the other customers.

The Jefferson Grill rapidly became a popular hangout in the neighborhood, and my grandfather and his larger-than-life personality became well known along with it.

He spoke broken English and knew he didn't always know the right word for things, but he used that and his sense of humor to joke around with customers as well as poking fun at his own shortcomings.

He became well respected for his ability to run a business. People would often ask him to borrow money, and he would answer by slowly pulling his wallet from his back pocket.

He would study the inside: "I no see the five dollars in here you borrow last week," he would say. "So, I think I canna give you any more money until you pay me."

My grandfather also frequently told jokes, and this was one of his favorites:

> A man had trouble with his English, so his friend taught him how to say, "Apple pie and coffee," so when on the job, he could order some

food at the local restaurant during his lunch hour. This was fine with our man, and he was grateful to his friend, but after several months he wanted a little more variety in his fare. His friend was glad to oblige and taught him how to say, "Ham and cheese sandwich."

The man proudly walked into the restaurant the next day and said to the waitress, "Ham and cheese sandwich."

To which the waitress responded, "White, whole wheat, or rye?"

With shoulders sagging and the smile gone from his face, he answered back, "Apple pie and coffee."

When men, including my dad and uncle, returned from World War II, the bar became even more popular, and my grandfather started to expand his business. He would eventually own four bars and a few rental houses and a few other parcels of land.

After returning from the war, my father went off to college to study accounting. He was at Penn State University, attending using his G.I. Bill.

My grandfather called and asked him to come home, to help him run the now expanding bar.

Dad's funds were running low. The G.I. Bill was not what it is now, but even so, he was unsure. He really wanted to graduate.

The more he thought about it, the more plus sides he saw to going home. My dad finally gave in and agreed to come back and quit school.

My Uncle Tom was also home from the war, and the pair went to work for my grandfather. The bar prospered well into the 1950s and beyond. My grandfather, doing very well by that point, spoiled my grandmother with furs, clothes, and jewelry. Perhaps he was making up for the years he was so strict with her household allowance.

My dad always regretted not getting his degree in accounting, although he loved the bar and his business, he later realized that it was the biggest mistake of his life, which he could not have known. There was no predicting that what was once a thriving business would disintegrate due to the deteriorating neighborhood and ruin their livelihood as a result. My dad and Uncle Tom were not only brothers-in-law, but best friends, as close as brothers, and my dad often told me in over seventy years' time, they never once had a fight, including all the years they partnered together in their business at the bar.

They would often joke with my grandfather, and patrons would often bring in unusual gifts for him.

Once a customer who had been out hunting brought in a rabbit. My dad and uncle wrapped it in paper and put it on ice behind the bar, intending to give it to my grandfather later.

The bar got busy, and they either forgot or deliberately played a prank on him, I'm not sure which.

A 1950's ad from our local Democrat and Chronicle newspaper in Rochester, NY, advertising a New Year's Eve party at my grandfather's, and later my dad's and uncle's bar, The Jefferson Grill. The bar often hosted special events, dinners, parties, fish fries, and even had "floor shows" and dancing girls!

Papa Joe Now Sings Lullabys at Night

Joe DiProspero, better known as "Little Joe" of the Jefferson Grill, is currently serenading his neighbors on Marilou Dr.

Seems that Joe and his Missus now have a cute little 8½ pound baby girl by the name of Diane to cuddle. We join with everyone else in wishing the new parents and their daughter the best of everything in the years to come.

Customers of my dad's bar and neighbors from Marilou Drive got together and posted this announcement of my adoption and "homecoming." Everyone who knew my parents knew how long they had waited to be parents and were aware my mom lost a baby ten years before I was born. Everyone was so thrilled and supportive; and I was so blessed to come home to such a loving family.

Either way, my grandfather started serving drinks at the bar and reached down without looking to grab some ice.

Instead of cold ice cubes, he felt warm fur.

He jumped nearly six feet in the air and brought the house down with laughter, which he joined good-naturedly. That was my grandfather.

There were events that changed Jefferson Avenue and the bar forever.

On June 24, 1964, at a dance on Nassau Street near Jefferson Avenue, police with dogs arrested a young African American man. He was 19, intoxicated, and resisted arrest. Onlookers protested the level of violence the police used to restrain him and inserted themselves into the fight. They threw bricks and bottles at the police, things escalated, and by three the next morning, the city had declared a state of emergency.

Racial tensions rose, looting and violence erupted, and Rochester made the national news. The riots, while mostly concentrated in the 7th ward, spread to the 3rd and 5th Ward, and even to Central Park to the south.

Due to the increasing violence, my dad and uncle had no choice but to carry guns to their business for their own protection. The neighborhood remained unstable. The state police were called in. Governor Nelson Rockefeller called in the National Guard. Cars were overturned, buildings were vandalized, and windows were broken. Bricks were hurled, bottles and cans were thrown at police, and other objects were used as weapons.

But the people in the area respected my grandfather, and his building remained unscathed through the height of the protests.

By the time the disturbance was over, four people were dead, three from a police helicopter crash. Three hundred and fifty people were injured, nearly a thousand arrests were made, and over two hundred stores were looted or damaged.

Dick Baumbach, a reporter for ABC, had a bullet graze his cheek, and one police officer lost an eye to a bottle.

The riot was blamed by many on outside agitators, but most of the rioters arrested were from the area, so the rumors turned out to be untrue.

The rioting was considered under control by August 3rd. The National Guard and State Police left, and the city police took over. Even though there was no physical damage to his bar, and no one was hurt, my grandfather suffered deep disappointment. Times had changed, and he felt like it was time to move on.

Losing the family business would impact all their financial futures for sure, but the city of Rochester and the beloved Jefferson Bar and Grill were caught in the crossfire of a race relations war and made the national news for all the wrong reasons.

In 1966, they sold the bar, and my dad and uncle moved on to other jobs. My grandfather was seventy-two at the time, already retired.

In the decade following the riots, the city acquired much of the land where the events occurred, leveled many of the buildings, and removed or repositioned streets, making the area almost unrecognizable.

Downtown Rochester had changed permanently.

But my dad had come a long way already, and he was a strong man. Which was a good thing because he had a long way to go.

My grandfather died seven years later, in 1973, at the age of 79, on the eve of my 11th birthday. My cousin, Tony, his only grandson, was born on Grandpa Baldo's birthday. We were the only two grandchildren on my mother's side of the family. I, of course, had no idea this small coincidence would only be the tip of the iceberg in terms of signs and unfathomable mysteries the Universe would have in store for my life.

Chapter Fourteen: The Suit

A year after they sold the bar, in 1967 I believe, my dad and I sat in the front seat of the car. He held my five-year-old hand tightly. The radio was on, and my dad either sang or whistled along as we drove.

A warm breeze came through the open windows. I rode up front next to him often on errands or visits to friends and relatives. I felt protected and loved, and my heart was happy and full. Being in his presence lit my soul, and I could see his joy at the opportunity to spend time with me.

On this day, we were headed to visit a friend of my father, and we visited this man fairly often, especially my dad did, with and without me present. They met under what may seem like odd circumstances to us, but that were quite common at the time. After his wife passed, my dad's father often took in boarders to make a little extra money. One of them was the man we were now headed to visit, a man named Vincent D'Raimo.

Although they'd met when my father was just a youth, he'd stayed friends with his man, and years later, now 42, my father was still loyal to him.

I remember the house clearly, not just for how it looked, but how it made me feel. Just looking at it, I felt sadness, loneliness, and a sense of hopelessness.

And it was no wonder. There seemed no real reason for the house to stay together such was its state of decay. Inside, non-descript linoleum, the color of oatmeal gone black was uneven everywhere and creaked as we walked across it. We passed through what was once a dining room but looked like it had been transferred there from the television show *Dark Shadows.*

A generation of dust had given birth to a second generation, the family of filth living on ancient dark mahogany furniture. Intricate designs decorated the drawers, and despite the coating of dirt, it was still ornate and beautiful.

A large dresser sat against one wall, used as a makeshift hutch, registered as out of place even to my young mind.

My eyes darted to my father's face, asking him the question: "What happened here?" The words my young mind could not articulate were, "Why is this place so forlorn, dirty, and broken?"

My father squeezed my hand, answering without speaking. "It's okay. I'm here with you. Everything is fine."

My tiny insides churned with uncertainty, but I trusted I was safe with my dad.

The area beyond the dining room was protected by a sheer piece of fabric hung in an arched doorway. My dad pushed it back slightly, careful not to pull it down, and revealed a bedroom.

Vincent lay there. He was in his seventies, I would guess now, but looked a decade beyond that. Sunken cheeks sprouted a scruffy beard. Patches of white hair decorated the top and sides of his head. His front teeth were long gone, and his hands were folded over a swollen stomach clad in a dirty white tank top, one often referred to as a "wife-beater." The air was musty, the scent coming from grey and tan blankets covering the bottom half of his body.

A nightstand sat on one side of the bed. A table on the other side held an oval shaving mirror, a razor, and a large bowl of water. Next to that, a shaving brush and cream waited patiently.

After greeting each other in Italian, my dad and his friend continued their conversation in the language I didn't understand. I waited quietly, not daring to move. I just stared on in awe.

Vincent's voice was filled with gravel. My father set a package of Italian cookies down on his nightstand. Another bag, filled with fresh peaches and pears, joined it.

They talked for a bit longer. I stared at my dad as if to say, "Let's get out of here."

He looked back, with a glance that said all I needed to hear: "We're not leaving yet, be patient."

So, I sat, waited, and watched.

My dad asked Vincent a question and then slid some shaving items, including a large bowl filled with water on a nightstand table closer to his friend. With the brush, he lathered Vincent's face with the shaving cream, and with the straight razor, he shaved his beard.

I could see Vincent relax. He seemed to drift into another world, perhaps another time and place that brought him comfort. I watched as my father worked quickly but didn't rush. His hands moved methodically and gently.

He washed Vincent's face when he was done, and the old man looked refreshed and renewed in his body and in his spirit. His formerly dead eyes sparkled.

My insides relaxed too as he and my father talked. His now rosy cheeks jiggled with laughter.

He swung his legs out from under the covers. I don't remember if I just turned around on my own or my dad told me to, while he assisted Vincent in putting on his trousers.

My dad's friend insisted that we follow him, and I think my father asked where we were going. He didn't answer, just motioned for us to follow. My father grabbed my hand, and we did, through the dining room where we scared clouds of dust from their resting places until they settled once more after our passing.

He hunched as he walked, and his gait was slow. My father reached out to steady him and asked in Italian if he was okay.

Vincent turned and growled at him, and my father responded with something I was sure meant, "Okay, walk by yourself then."

We exited through the sagging front door. The driveway consisted of broken up cement. Weeds poked their heads stubbornly through every crack, and crumbs of concrete decorated the ground.

We headed toward a little patch of ground that could have been called a backyard if it was maintained as such. Before we got there, we reached a group of tall plants, and the elderly man reached up and cut off a bunch of Italian grapes from them, the ones used to make wine. They were sour and slimy to eat, but oddly good anyway. It was the only thing he had to offer us, and he smiled his toothless grin as my father took them and thanked him profusely.

He then turned his attention to me and pulled a couple of crumpled dollar bills from his pocket.

My father protested, Vincent growled, and I took them. I said, "Thank you," and the two men turned to say their goodbyes. The giving of the dollar bills was always the sign our visit had ended.

My father offered to help Vincent back inside, earning another growl and a refusal. His face seemed to resume its old hopelessness at the prospect of us leaving.

He waved as we left.

As I grew older, I would no longer go with my father on these visits. There was a housekeeper of sorts who lived upstairs from him. Heavyset, hair graying, she wore old house dresses, did not join in our visits, and seemed to be annoyed by having to care for Vincent.

She would call our house on his behalf when he wanted a visit from my father. This would happen at all times of the day and night, and my dad would go when he could.

About four years later, when I was nine, the calls got more frequent. My parents bickered over it, my dad hunched over the kitchen sink, his head in his hands, obviously distressed and my mother seeking to be appeased.

He was already working two jobs, one during the day, the other bartending two or three nights a week. On those nights, he would get a scant few hours' sleep.

My mother saw him pulled in many different directions. Vincent was just one more, another thing that took time away from her and us. Although she felt bad for Vincent, she felt my father should take care of himself before taking on the additional responsibility the old man brought.

My father would not budge. His friend needed him. We all did, and he could not be there for all of us, all the time.

The years went on. I would later notice a dark suit, brand new, hanging in our front coat closet. My father never wore it, nor did I ask about it, although I don't know why. It was covered in a plastic bag, to protect it, I was sure.

When I got much older, I realized what, or rather who the suit was for. My dad purchased it for the time when Vincent would pass away and wanted him to have it for a proper burial. The man had never married, had no children, and no living relatives we knew of.

The suit was his final gift to his friend.

My father did not teach me compassion through lessons in a book. He showed it to me, and he lived it. I observed it and experienced it from him. These things left an imprint on my heart that has lasted my entire life.

My maternal grandparents also taught me these lessons through showing kindness, right up until the time when they passed.

Chapter Fifteen: "O Solo Mio"

It was August 30, 1973. My maternal grandfather, Anthony, would die the next day, although I didn't know that yet.

My grandparents, Anthony and Angelina, Papa and Grandma, lived right down the street from me, and we had a close bond even when I was young. In the winter, they would stay in the home my grandfather built for them in Miami Beach. When there, my grandmother would send cards and letters to the whole family, and I treasured them. They were often written in flowery language, almost silly due to her ineptitude with written English. I admired her even more as I grew older for her determination to teach herself. She would sit with the dictionary by the hour to try to learn how to spell and write new vocabulary words and grasp their meaning.

Dad and Mom often visited my grandparents at Matheson Hammock Park beach in Miami, 1950s. How they loved this place!

Every now and then, I would be able to go to their Miami home with my mom and dad or my mom and her sisters to escape the frigid Rochester winters. I loved that time with them.

"The gang's all here!"

Top: My cousin Tony. Second row: my mom's twin Aunt Frances, Aunt Millie, and my mom. Bottom row: Grandpa Baldo, me, and Grandma Angelina. Missing from the photo are my dad and Uncle Tom. We were celebrating my grandparents' return from wintering at their home in Miami Beach. I was always so thrilled when they came back to Rochester for the summer and Fall.

But this night, my grandfather sat in a wheelchair, his thin face twisted, looking much like the actor William Edward Hickey from the movie *Prizzi's Honor*. He sang his favorite song to us: "O Solo Mio."

It was heart-wrenching to see him in this condition. My grandpa, Tony, had suffered several heart attacks over the previous few years, and they had been followed by a significant stroke that left him partially paralyzed. He'd spent many months in a nearby nursing home trying, through rehab, to get strong enough so we could bring him home.

My grandparents had enough money, my grandmother was able to bring him home and get physical therapists to come to the house, something almost unheard of in the early 70s.

But this night, my previously rotund grandpa looked nothing like he did prior to his stroke. He'd lost at least eighty pounds. He spent many days in a coma, and we barely recognized him.

The very fact that he came out of the coma, considering the primitive care available for stroke victims at the time, and lived for a couple more years, was not lost on any one of us. He was happy and jovial that evening, and our family shared his joy.

But early the next morning he told my grandmother he was not feeling well but insisted she not call the doctor. She found him in his favorite recliner chair, his face was cold and clammy. I remember her telling me she was calm, but obviously devastated at the loss. One look told her he was gone. He passed away on August 31, 1973, my 11th birthday.

From that point until she passed away when I was in my late thirties, my grandmother continued to be a guiding force and loving presence for me, my family, and my kids.

We were close, but not in the way grandparents sometimes are nowadays. We didn't go bowling, to movies, roller skating, or camping together. My grandparents rarely babysat me, as my aunts served that role.

Instead, they were old-school Italian grandparents. We talked. My grandmother and I cooked and baked together. We spent many Sundays eating large dinners, and we spent our holidays together. We formed a very close bond, and I knew I was loved and cherished by both of them.

They were the head of our family and treated as such. My grandmother continued the role on her own after my grandfather passed away. She kept an immaculate house, always spotless no matter when I dropped by. I would often ride my bike up the street and just pop in.

There was always something delicious simmering on the stove, home-cooked soup or stew, and the smell was intoxicating. In typical Italian fashion, she offered me food constantly.

Even though she was rather "big-boned" as my family often described her, she didn't look like a typical Italian woman. Her snow-white hair, fair complexion, and blue eyes didn't match her heritage. She wore what were commonly called "house dresses," cotton, short-sleeved, and with a checkered pattern. They were usually light in color, and she wore them belted at her waist. She wore stockings and low-heeled dress shoes. I never saw her wear pants.

When she dressed up for special occasions, she wore the finest of ladies' dresses or suits, complete with pearls or diamonds. Her face would be "made up" with her Estee Lauder makeup, topped with perfume. The combination meant she always smelled like powder and roses.

My grandmother was sweet, loving, and she had a great sense of humor. She constantly worried about my mother, her illness, and the impact it had on me. I often saw her wringing her hands, tears forming in her eyes, looking hopeless and helpless. She would often rant that "those twins," referring to my mother and her sister Frances, were going to kill her with their bad behavior.

I can't imagine the stress she went through, but she would hug me and offer comfort the many times I was upset with either of them. There were many of those times, I am sorry to say.

But that's what grandparents do, and having her there to understand, to try to offer me reassurance, and comfort me did take some of the sting out of the hell happening at my house.

I enjoyed a lot of happy and fun times with her. Armed with only a third-grade education, she still wanted to be a proper lady. She showed us proper manners, etiquette, and how to be classy and gentle. She entertained family and friends and set tables with fine china and Italian linens that could compete with royalty. Her love and kindness were of great value to me.

Perhaps one of the funniest memories I have of her, and one of the most important, was a lesson she taught me about the birds and the bees.

Chapter Sixteen: The Birds and the Bees

On a not so ordinary day, my grandmother tried to explain sex to me.

I was ten, and my grandfather wasn't around, or I'm sure the conversation would have never happened. It was before his death, so he may have been in the nursing home still or just sleeping.

But my maternal grandmother, who gave me ordinary days, who often rescued me from my mother's addiction and the chaos at home, now sat with me at her dining room table. She wore a pearl or gold necklace, and I could smell her smell, powder and roses.

She leaned in close, and the action felt almost menacing.

She was about to teach me about the birds and the bees. This was something Italian grandmothers meant business about: it was her job to intimidate me and teach me that although sex wasn't to be feared, it was mysterious.

Words came from her mouth, but I did not even know what sex was.

"Do you know what a virgin is?" she asked. There was a single important point to the lesson she wanted to share today.

I think I might have nodded, and swallowed hard, although I don't remember if I did or not. She went on to explain some things.

"Have I made myself perfectly clear?" she said as she finished.

She had not, but I pretended to understand. I was confused, scared of the very ideas she had presented, and embarrassed. I certainly didn't want to smile, let alone ask questions.

She went on to emphasize our Italian culture, and how a person should act. That sex was mysterious, and sacred to marriage because of our family values and our Catholic faith. These were the lessons she tried to impart.

She wanted to teach me, to help me know and understand about fear and shame, the Catholic rule keepers.

"This is the way a young lady conducts herself," she explained. "Do you understand what not being a virgin means?" she asked again.

By this time, I might have, but I nodded.

Ignoring my gesture, she continued, "You know that if you are not a virgin when you get married, Diana, you cannot—" She took a deep breath and leaned closer. This was the point of the entire lesson.

"You cannot walk down the aisle wearing a white veil. Not unless you are a virgin. You will burn in hell!"

I nodded vigorously. Whatever that meant, to be a virgin on your wedding day, I wanted to be that.

Sweet baby Jesus, I thought to myself. *If I am not a virgin when I get married, I will have to wear a black wedding dress and veil, or none at all. The whole world will know why I cannot wear white. I can never let his fate befall me.*

I pledged to her right then and there to be a good girl.

She nodded. I knew she was saying, as she often did when we were cooking, talking about dressing, or other family traditions: "This is the way we do."

It would certainly be the way I did things.

Chapter Seventeen: The Mall and Rabbit Stew

There is one thing that if you don't by now, you must understand. My mom's illness, the dysfunction I often suffered at home, meant that ordinary days often held special meaning for me.

My grandparents provided both ordinary days and extraordinary ones for me. That's probably why I remember a June day in 1970 so well.

"C'mon, Diana, let's go," my grandfather called to me. They often called me "Diana."

I ran to join them. It was summer-hot. I felt protected and calm.

This was before his strokes. His round face slicked back black and white hair, and smiling eyes told me he was up to something good. He wore the things I remember him wearing most often, black-ish trousers, a white short-sleeved dress shirt. He might have been wearing what many would call the "Italian man costume," a ribbed, white tank top tucked into belted dress pants.

I remember the little garden in their back yard, a source of tomatoes and peppers, and although I could picture him watering it, that is not where we were going.

Instead, we piled into my grandfather's olive-green Buick LeSabre, a 1968 giant of a car. He slid behind the wheel, my grandmother filled the passenger seat with her smile, clad in her yellow and white checked house dress.

"Where are we going?" I asked. I don't think they told me, but I was happy just to be with them.

My grandparents cranked down the huge front windows, and the breeze washed over me in the backseat, cooling my face.

Once we were on the road, they spoke of a beautiful new mall that had opened, our destination. Grandmother wanted to go to Sears and get a new washing machine, but to me, it simply felt like a big adventure.

It felt like we were on the road for an hour, but it was probably much shorter. The song "It's So Nice to Be with You" played on the radio, and I remember this day whenever I hear that song, because it was a rare, ordinary day, and I got to spend it with them.

Another day, perhaps that same summer, perhaps the next year, June, toward the end of the school year, the bus dropped me off a couple of doors down from my house. I lugged my clear plastic book bag, the kind with flowers on the outside, the handles threatening to break, toward the house. I labored to get it inside.

I wore a light jacket, left over from the cool morning, over my Catholic school jumper, navy cable-knit knee socks, my black but thin bangs blowing all over my face as I walked. The very day felt heavy, long, and challenging.

First, I was never a morning person to start with. As I have already shared, I was thin, had allergies, nosebleeds, and was constantly plagued with one stomach virus or another or a throat infection. I was a typical mealy-mouthed kid, always tired it seemed.

By the end of the day, I was disheveled, tired, and lugging that heavy book bag around. Even toward the end of the year, we were burdened with homework.

The short walk from the bus stop to home felt much longer than it was, and I walked between the two trees out front and diagonally across the meticulous front lawn, the grass still wet, all I could think of was dumping my book bag, changing clothes, and laying on my bed for a few minutes before I had to start my homework.

On days when things were good for her, my mother would have the most amazing after school snacks waiting for me. I never ate much for breakfast, the lunch period was short and rushed, and I would arrive home ravenous. She would have a tray of crudités, hard-boiled eggs, crackers, and cheese, or whatever else would fill my belly.

She would often greet me enthusiastically. Looking back, I feel bad for my initial grumpiness when I returned home. What was a highlight of her day was drudgery to me, until I could fill my belly, change clothes, and shed the cares of my day.

Most of these days, she would be watching her soap operas, and I would watch them with her as I ate.

This day was a bit different though. I entered through the breezeway and ascended the stairs toward the first floor of the house. I looked down into the basement, and my grandfather Tony stood there with a big smile on his face.

I could hear the rumble of the washer and dryer, and I heard my mom's voice, so I could tell she, too, was in the basement.

My grandfather raised his hand in a wave. "Diana! Diana! Come down here. I want to show you something."

I dropped my bag, and moved to run down the steps, I saw a tall cardboard box there.

A surprise.

"Come, come," he said, and I flew down the steps toward this man fast as I could. When I reached the bottom, he motioned for me to look inside.

There was a tiny white rabbit with the pinkest eyes I'd ever seen.

It was so beautiful, I nearly cried. I squealed and gave him the biggest hug. "A beautiful bunny, just for me?"

I wanted a rabbit, and here it was, courtesy of my mom and my grandfather.

"Fluffy" as I named her had a large crate in the corner of the kitchen of our small house, next to where the phone sat on the counter. I played with that rabbit all summer and I loved her. She was sweet, only nipping my fingers from time to time.

She grew and grew. I would take her out of her crate, and she would hop around our dining set, around the braided rug underneath. With a taste of freedom, she would head to the living room and hide behind the olive-green pattern on pattern sofa there.

Unable to catch her, I would lie in wait and finally grab her, returning her to her home.

Little did I know that the trips behind the couch included a bit of chewing on the lamp cords there and the depositing of little raisin-like rabbit gifts behind the sofa. She also left these on the braided rug under the dining room table.

My mother cleaned up after her, washed the rugs, discovered the frayed lamp cords, and worried. She worried the rabbit would get electrocuted not to mention the destruction of the cords.

Still, Fluffy grew, nearly too large for her cage now.

One day months later, I arrived home from school to find that Fluffy was gone.

My mother told me that the rabbit was too big to be happy here. She'd given her to Nick, the egg man, who delivered eggs and milk to us. He lived on a farm, she explained. Fluffy would have a better life, be with other rabbits, and have room to run and play.

Of course, I was devastated, but there was little I could do. My mother grew tired of cleaning up rabbit poop, and the rabbit had outgrown us. That was that.

Years later, I found out the truth.

My grandfather, who grew up in hard times, had once been a butcher. Where he grew up, you killed your own chickens and other fowl, and when the time came you slaughtered them and ate them.

Fluffy, far from living on a farm happily ever after, instead made her way to our table. Fluffy became rabbit stew.

This was so my grandfather and my family, and a typical series of events from my childhood!

Chapter Eighteen: Kaleidoscope

My childhood is like a kaleidoscope. Catholic grade school, Catholic high school, Sunday dinners, Sunday church, singing in the church choir, family vacations to the Adirondacks, always three days, not two, not four, that was all we could afford. We rode horses, played tennis, and swam in the giant in-ground pool at the resort.

Girl Scouts, piano lessons, guitar lessons, dancing lessons, parties, family picnics, where the old Italian women in their house dresses arrived at 8 a.m. and boiled large kettles of water for the pasta. We ate pasta or filet mignon or both from good china also carted out to the park. There were no hot dogs, not like other families. My surprise Sweet Sixteen party, thrown in combination with my then-boyfriend, friends, and parents, graduation parties, dinners out to fancy restaurants, trips to my grandparents' home in Florida, helping at the Dress Shoppe in the City where my aunt worked, working at Dunkin Donuts, my first official job: all of these were colors in the kaleidoscope.

There was the houseful of various pets growing up, poodle after poodle, birds, canaries, always named, what else: "Larry," my mother's idea. She loved the birds and my dad hated them. She overfed them with egg biscuits too, until they dropped over dead, and we would find them at the bottom of their cages.

There were sleepovers at my house with all my school girlfriends, summers riding my 10-speed Varsity bike all over town, never-ending hours doing homework from the Catholic schools I was fortunate enough to attend. School days, "riding in cars, with boys," college days, and finally meeting my husband the summer before college, dating for 5 years and marrying in September of 1985, at age 23.

When I look back on my life, it feels as though I didn't miss a trick. So much family, friends, *life,* was packed into my growing up years, despite my mom being very ill, in spite of dysfunction, addiction, depression, sickness, tight finances, etc.

My dad, aunts, uncle, and grandmother, neighborhood families, and my friends were instrumental in filling in the gaps when my mother couldn't be present for me, even though her illness was a taboo subject, and something I was forbidden to ever speak about to others.

"There was a little girl, who had a little curl,
Right in the middle of her forehead,
And when she was good, she was very, very good,
But when she was bad, she was horrid."

That was my mother! I've told you when my mother was well, life was grand. My grandparents were my solace, my grandmother, my comfort, even after my grandfather passed.

My aunts babysat me; my Aunt Millie helped to raise me during mom's rougher times.

Aunt Millie and Uncle Tom, my godparents, on my baptismal day. Always like "other parents" to me all my life. You can see that, even as an infant, I adored her, and him, too!

From my mother's Hallmark card-writing curses to the awful days hiding out from her, I was not allowed to speak of them. I coped. I barricaded myself in my bedroom, spending long, lonely periods reading and listening to music to drown out her verbal abuse.

Yet my life remained extraordinary. My dad and his family all pitched in to raise me when my mother could not be present.

There were things ingrained in me, things I could not forget. "Get a good education and work hard." I would soon develop my work ethic with my aunt's help, following in my father's footsteps. I went to work at LaMar's Dress Shoppe, where my aunt worked and even lived, when she and my uncle were first married. They stayed in a small apartment above the store.

Not only could I make a few dollars, but I would escape my mom's issues. It was a win-win.

The shop was located in an old, converted house in the city of Rochester, New York. If you walked all the way to the rear area, there was a sewing room with four sewing machines and a seamstress at each. They were Italian women who were masters at their trade. They'd each apprenticed in Italy before coming to New York.

The shop featured formal gowns and bridal dresses, along with some causal wear. The best part of the job was that I got to work with my beloved Aunt Millie, and I felt grown up and productive.

The latest bridal gowns were on display in the front window, and I became the window dresser, choosing the gowns to display and putting them on the mannequins each week. When not doing that, I folded cardboard boxes by the boatload, getting paid between a penny and a dime for each box.

Sometimes I was given a magnet and assigned to crawl around the dressing room and find the pins and needles the seamstresses might have dropped.

The room was shaped like a horseshoe. All the dresses hung around the perimeter of the shop, and a round platform sat in the center. This is where the brides would stand as the seamstresses took measurements and worked on the hems of their gowns.

Next to the checkout counter was a small jewelry display. Inside were necklaces, bracelets, and earrings that would make great accessories. I took it upon myself to arrange this display case, setting up the scarves, fake grapes, artificial flowers, and whatever I could to dress it up artfully. I received compliments from customers who noticed the display and bought more jewelry.

I loved working at LaMar's, and I often worked two evenings a week and a Saturday with my aunt when I was not consumed with other teenage activities.

As you walked to the sewing room, if you took a quick left, there was a kitchen. The shop owner, Nancy LaMartina's mother would often cook lunches for the dress shop staff. On Saturdays, there was always food. I would eat her pasta, sauce, eggplant, and other Italian dishes. I can still smell the tomatoes, garlic, and other spices emanating during those lunches.

However, once I started high school, studies took a priority, and my days at LaMar's were few.

One night, I was studying at home. Never a brilliant math student, I struggled with geometry. My stomach was in knots, and I feared I might not pass.

My aunt came by, off early from work for some reason, and checked up on me. She found me despondent, books and papers scattered over the floor of my room.

I'd worked myself up into a tizzy. I knew most times if I had a grasp on something, I would pass with a 90 or above, and be fine. But if I didn't understand it, I always feared I would fail, with no happy medium between.

Ever optimistic, my aunt tried to reassure me.

"Honey, you are smart, you will be fine. You got this."

I got angry with her, and I have no idea why. She was just trying to be positive.

"You don't understand. This is important to me. School is important to me. If I fail, I'll have to go to summer school."

"Oh, honey, you will be fine," she told me.

"I'm not going to summer school. I've never been, and I am not about to start."

She tried again to console me.

"What if LaMar's burned down tomorrow?" I said (to this day, I do not know what made me blurt out that statement). I did know how important the shop and her job were to her. She'd been working there for over forty years. "That is your whole life. Well, school is my whole life."

The next day, I got a call from her that some hoodlums had set fire to some boxes in the alley. LaMar's had been damaged beyond repair, and so she lost her long-time job.

I passed the geometry final with a grade of 83.

This was just one of my clairvoyant moments growing up.

It was a small slice, a section, of the kaleidoscope that was my life.

Chapter Nineteen: Marilou Drive

When I think back on my life, my growing up years and my history, no story of my life and my family could ever be complete without a mention of my neighborhood and the street I grew up on in Rochester, in the Town of Gates, New York, Marilou Drive.

I often recall my dad telling me how the builder at the time, named it for his daughter, "Mary Lou," changed the "Y" to an "I," and combined the two names.

My parents built their home sometime around 1955, before they adopted me, in 1962. My grandparents already had moved from their "city neighborhood" on Jefferson Avenue, near my grandfather's bar and later, Jay Street.

This move, in my estimation, could be likened to the popular TV sitcom, *The Jeffersons*. Although *The Jeffersons* was about a black family escaping the city and moving to a better neighborhood, the theme of "movin' on up" applies to their experience as well. A move to build a home, even a small, ranch-style home in the suburbs was a sign of financial upward movement in the world.

I vividly remember the stories of hearing how proud they were!

As for me, I was brought home at six weeks old, when I was adopted and released, I am told, from a foster home to my parents and my home on Marilou Dr. Whatever my house was or wasn't, I didn't even have a real understanding of my neighborhood until at least age 5 or 6.

I do recall my mother, aunts, and grandmother working tirelessly, or so it seemed, cleaning, dusting, vacuuming, washing clothes, ironing, and even "waxing" their furniture, kitchen cupboards, and linoleum floors, as was the custom in those days.

I remember the smell of Easy-off spray starch, bleach, lemon Pledge and the mothballs they put in closets to keep the clothes "fresh." Our house always smelled so beautiful and clean.

For having just a handful of small rooms, it seemed it was all my mom, aunts and grandmother could do to keep up with it all. Not sure why it was so much labor, or if they just made more work for themselves than it had to be. I do know they had tons of pride in their little homes and tried to keep them as perfect as humanly possible. They took the job of being wives, mothers, and housekeepers very seriously.

Looking back now, I realize what an iconic neighborhood and period of history I was fortunate enough to have grown up in. Such an age of innocence, privacy, and perhaps dashes of ignorance, naivete, secrecy, pride, good morals, humor, and hard-working middle-class folks.

I was surrounded by a slice of truly iconic Americana. It is the stuff that *The Wonder Years* TV show was made of. The neighborhood itself was not at all diverse. It was predominately white, Italian, with a few German families, and one Jewish family who we all loved and drew into our circle. Almost every adult on my street I addressed as "Aunt so-and-so" or "Uncle so-and-so." I never questioned this lifestyle, and just thought of these wonderful neighbors as extended family.

Even at a very tender age, I realized that these people were not actually all my "aunts" and "uncles," but I also understood, without it ever really being explained to me, that I was to address them that way out of respect. Later, as I grew and got to know and love them, it was out of pure affection!

Neither did I experience any families with divorced parents, gay parents, or any other family situation that did not consist of two parents and their children. The only exception, which I gave zero thought to, and it never occurred to me that it was a different situation was my mother's twin sister, who, by the time I was in the picture was divorced and lived in a house diagonally across the street from where I did.

I am not sure I can ever do Marilou Drive the justice it deserves in a few short pages. The neighbors didn't always get together at everyone's house. It wasn't exactly that way. We didn't have what some people would call block parties or even picnics. But everyone knew everyone. Everyone was friendly. It *felt* like a family to me. Kids rode their bikes up and down its uneven cement sidewalks. There were no streetlights. Neighbors sometimes walked up and down, too. People respected each other's privacy. But, if someone were sick or in the hospital, everyone brought food or called to check in. Everyone smiled and waved as they drove past your house.

That was part of my experience of the two worlds on Marilou Drive: my internal world, of my own house and family, and the external world of all the other families that lived around us who I came to know and love so dearly, but especially three of them: The Guerras, the Sciascias and the Padulos.

I was in and out of a lot of the houses, because of my neighborhood friends. And these three families will always be in my heart and soul, and they shaped me into who I am.

The Guerras had four daughters, Angela, Frances, Josephine, or "JoJo" as we called her, and Annette. They were just about like the older sisters I never had but always longed for. I addressed their parents as "Aunt Lee and Uncle Louie." They took me in and treated me like their "fifth daughter."

They often bought me beautiful dresses and gifts for my birthdays and Christmas, despite having four kids of their own, and I was a fixture at their house and dinner table. Often my embarrassed mother, who felt certain I had overstayed my welcome, would come over to fetch me and drag me home.

I had such fun at their house and became closest to their youngest daughter, Annette, who was five years older than me, a big age difference when you are young. Nevertheless, I hung around and ingratiated myself with their family, and admired and looked up to Annette. Of course, I wanted to be just like her; dress like her, listen to the music she listened to. It seemed I would sit hours on end in her psychedelic, 70s style bedroom watching wide-eyed as my friend made up her face with eyeliner and more, to go on dates with boys. It was all so mysterious and magical to me! And I wanted to be just like her. In fact, it was kind of a joke because I knew, even at that age, the adults were all watching me, and how much I was trying to emulate her and copy everything she did.

Her parents brought me everywhere: out for ice cream in the summer with their daughter, to many church carnivals and festivals, and even to their brother's and sister's houses when they went to visit. I was in my glory, and all the experiences with my neighbor families enriched my life greatly. I was just like a tiny sponge, taking in every experience I possibly could. It felt like a magical carpet ride to my young mind, and time became non-existent. I went everywhere with the Guerras.

Because of my dad's rigorous work schedule and my mom's illness, a part of my desire to escape my house was for fun and new experiences, but another part was survival. Having these families around helped me learn so many things and escape the boredom and fear I experienced at times at home, alone with my sick mother.

Not only was I a very inquisitive and social being from a very young age, but I was determined to have fun and make my life a good one.

The other families were my next-door neighbors, the Sciascia family who had three sons, Sam, Richard[1] and Carl, and a daughter, Frances, whom I adored. They all treated me, again, like a member of their family and showered me with love and affection. Richard happened to be my cousin Tony's best friend. Tony was thirteen years older than me, my Aunt Frances's son. I was mesmerized by all the teenagers.

Tony had a penchant for fast muscle cars. He even built himself a dragster, in my aunt's basement. Then later, had to disassemble it to get it upstairs, and then he promptly rebuilt it in her garage! He took me for a ride in it, racing up and down Marilou Drive. More than one of our wonderful neighbors disapproved of its thunderous roar.

My Aunt Frances often had a houseful of teenagers, and she would cook different meals and snacks. Even though she lived on a shoestring budget, my grandparents supported her, because she was unable to work. Even so, she was never happier than

---

[1] Richard Sciascia, my long-time next-door neighbor and friend to so many in Rochester, New York, was sadly and tragically shot and killed on April 7, 2021, in a string of car-jackings, leaving our community forever changed, saddened, and heartbroken. Edgar Tolentino, aged 16, was later charged in his murder.

when my cousin and all his teenage friends and "grease monkeys" were hanging out at her house.

The boys often hung out in the garage, under this car or that car, whatever my cousin and his friends were tinkering with. I have only the haziest of memories of this, as I must have been between the ages of about 4 and 8 years old and remember kind of being shooed away by my cousin and his friends.

Many summer nights, warm and breezy, and full of possibilities and excitement, my mother would come across the street, much to my dismay, to fetch me and bring me home. My little mind registered that anything could happen. It would be bath time, time to get into pajamas, and then I was allowed to watch one show on television.

It was usually *The Monkeys,* with Davy Jones, whom I adored. By 8 p.m., when it was still light out, my heavy drapes on my bedroom window blew back and forth with the summer breeze as I climbed into my canopy bed. I often had difficulty falling asleep, but I was forced to go to bed and stay in bed.

Out of my window, kitty-corner, across the street, I could still see my Aunt Frances's house and wonder with longing what all those teenagers were doing and why I couldn't stay and have fun with them.

The other family I grew very close to the Padulo family and their kids, Richard and Lori. Both were several years younger than me. Their house wasn't technically on Marilou Drive, but it was situated (from the backyards) to the side of Aunt Frances' house and just around the corner on busy Brooks Ave, which also had no sidewalks. Their kids would cut through my aunt's backyard and walk their bikes out a few yards onto Marilou Drive.

Growing up, my friends were either four or five years older than me, or four or five years younger than me. Richard and Lori became like best friends to me as well. They even took me a couple of times to their mobile home in the Thousand Islands, Alexandria Bay area, where I got to water ski.

I often wondered growing up if Richard and Lori were more like friends or like a little brother and sister. I ended up babysitting for them a few times as we grew older. Their parents were very close to me and my family, and now looking back, I never did address their parents as "Aunt Maryann" and "Uncle Richard" and I'm not sure why.

Maryann was the neighborhood hairdresser who did the hair of most of the ladies who lived around us. My family went every Friday. She had a little shop annexed to the backside of her house which served as a small salon. I spent many summer afternoons there, in the backyard playing or in their finished basement. I also was there for many dinners and parties of all kinds. They later bought the first Skidoo I had ever seen, and took me, along with their kids, snowmobiling in the open fields next to their house.

This chapter of my life wouldn't be complete without a mention of all my neighborhood friends whom I loved, adored and influenced me and spent lots of time with including the Volonino family, Alice, Danny, whose dad, Tony, was one of my dad's best friends, and my very close and best friend, Linda Creamer and all her brothers, too.

As the years went on, and I knew more and more of the families and neighbors. Rumors and stories of the older kids and their escapades both good and naughty filtered to me seemingly by "osmosis." My listening skills combined with the neighborhood grapevine, adults' conversations, and I can only assume a radar I developed to "sniff out information" enabled me to gather these things "in the wind." I have no other way to explain the awareness I gained of much of the "goings-on" of the families, and the teenagers on that street.

I also knew it was "top-secret stuff" and that I was never "supposed to know" these things. I kept many secrets to myself. Secrecy was the unspoken codeword of the day. It was just a given, as the secret of my mother's illness. Without question, I clung to this code, never questioning, and never, ever breaking it, to or for anyone.

Remember: there was no social media back then. Also, the neighbors kept a respectful distance. Yet, there was still somehow a feeling of community and connectedness that is hard, if not impossible to describe.

I remember my mother in the backyard, hanging clothes on a line with clothespins and talking to neighbors on either side of chain link fences, I recall my dad waving at and having conversations with neighbors both to the left and right of our house and in our backyard—straight behind us and to either side. The people who lived on the street behind us, the Lomando family and the Gorevskis who immigrated from Yugoslavia, lived on what was known as "Sprucewood Lane," the street just behind Marilou Drive. We were also friends with them, and their daughter Anita became my friend by talking over the fence! Many decades-long friendships were conceived in those days over those chain-link fences.

I would also go to Anita's and she would come to my house. Through the Gorevskis, who did not speak English, I was treated to Yugoslavian cooking, which I absolutely loved. They had a huge vegetable garden and would sometimes give peppers and tomatoes to my parents. The Gorevskis even took me to their orthodox church festivals and bought me clothes because I adored Anita, and tried to emulate her too, another friend a few years older than myself.

Years passed. We grew up, the neighborhood kids went to college, moved out, and got married. A few of them have even passed away now. My friend Anita died of lung cancer in 2004.

Sadly, almost every original neighbor (well, at least, the parents that were around my dad's age) from that neighborhood is now deceased. Most of my friends are, thankfully, still living. My dad struggled mightily with these losses. Not only did he lose his parents when he was a child, Dad also suffered the loss of his siblings, many at very young ages, then friends, other relatives, my mother in 2003 and, one by one, those cherished neighbors from good, old Marilou Drive.

My dad was one of the last to pass away of the original group to move to that sweet, humble street. The loss of those wonderful neighbors pained him more than I can ever describe because my dear father loved these people, this community, as if they, too, were family.

His losses seemed to pile up one after the other, and if each of us lives to be old, this is something we all must experience, of course. I was always in awe of the resilience and positivity he was determined to hang onto. I am sure this demeanor he exhibited, he intended not only to help himself but to lead by example, another gift I have no doubt he meant for me.

Marilou Drive remains in my heart forever, and a day.

Chapter Twenty: Meatballs, Sausage, and Fishing Tackle

There is one other hero in my story who cannot go without being thanked nor mentioned. It was the summer of 1980 and a friend of mine knew I was not working and asked me to help at a local store doing inventory. I could make a few dollars and since college would be starting soon, I agreed. I began the exciting job of counting and sorting of all things—fishing tackle!

The store was a well-known catalog showroom, called Naum Brothers, popular in the early 1980s. It sold a variety of items from small appliances to sporting goods and jewelry. Customers could browse in the store or in the catalog. To make a purchase they would fill out the shelf catalog item number on a slip of paper and take it to the back of the store where they would hand it to an employee. The merchandise was stored near a loading dock, taken off a conveyor belt, and carried to the cash register. Stores like this one were truly unique, but now have been replaced by online shopping.

Just thinking of this old-time era type of store makes me smile now.

This particular summer, I got quite a surprise gift from that catalog showroom in Rochester, New York.

One hot day lounging around my house, I stuck my head outside. I was barefoot, wearing jean shorts and a tube top. I walked out onto my front lawn when suddenly I heard my neighbor, Paulie. He was about ten years older than me, and his parents were good friends of my family. He was kind of a big brother to me from the time I was a little girl. He affectionately called me Meatball and I called him Sausage. Corny as this was, we thought nothing of it.

This was a part of life on Marilou Drive.

"Hey, Meatball!"

"Hey, Sausage," I called back.

I walked over to where Paulie was washing his car in the driveway. The Braccis lived on the other side of our house and we were sandwiched between them and the Sciascia family. My dad was also very close with his dad, Angelo, and mom, Juliette and their Aunt Mary lived in the house with them, upstairs. Another typical, loving Italian family. Paulie also happened to be another of my cousin Tony's close buddies. All part of his Marilou Drive clique of friends.

It was a really hot July day. He was soaping up his car, scrubbing and washing it with a sponge, and then hosing it down. "How's it going?" he asked.

"Good, Paulie, and you?" I responded.

"Hey, you got a boyfriend?" he asked.

Just then, the phone rang in my "Italian garage," as we called it.

My dad knocked out a wall years earlier, the one that separated the breezeway from the garage. He had a concrete floor poured, and he bought a screen for the garage to be used in summer months in place of the garage door. He furnished this room with discarded office furniture from Xerox, where he worked at the time. 1 can still picture the orange leather couch and chairs. He placed a tan speckled area rug over the cement floor. Inside the room was a wooden picnic table with benches. An uncle of mine installed a drop ceiling and paneled the walls. Adorning the walls were some of my drawings and various religious artifacts. To complete this new rec room was a refrigerator. Voila! Our Italian garage!

The phone was an old green rotary one which sat on a small white wrought-iron table near the kitchen door, and it emitted a ringing I could not ignore.

"I gotta go, Paulie. The telephone is ringing," I chirped as I flew across the yard, over the hot asphalt driveway, barefoot. I stepped through the old breezeway door into the garage and 1 grabbed the receiver from the cradle.

I did not want to miss this call or any call. There were no cell phones then, so every call was critical.

"Hello?" I gasped, out of breath from running.

"Hi," said the voice on the other end.

"Who's this?" I asked tentatively, even though I knew the answer.

"It's Rick," said the voice.

We chatted awhile. Rick was a friend of one of my best friends, Michelle. He was the guy I had just spent the weekend working with, counting the fishing tackle. When we ended our call, I skipped back across the lawn to Paulie.

My wedding day, September 6, 1985,
St. Helen's Church, Rochester, NY.

Rick and me at our wedding, September 6, 1985, at Sweet's Party House, in Rochester (Webster) New York. That cake was a masterpiece, made by local Savoia's bakery. My parents gave us the most amazing wedding, complete with ice sculpture, sit-down dinner, a live band, and fabulous sweets table! These things were pretty rare in 1985!

"Remember what you just asked me?" I asked. "If I had a boyfriend?"

"Yeah," he answered.

"Well, the answer is yes," I responded. "Yes, I do!"

Five years later l would marry Rick, my best friend, the man who has never let me down and who has given me two beautiful daughters. Rick is the man who has infinite patience with me and has loved and still loves me in sickness and in health as we stated in our marriage vows.

He's helped me care for all of my family, especially in the sad and horrible times in which I said goodbye to every one of them. With him by my side, we endured the heart-wrenching ordeal of burying every one of them.

Rick and I have been through so much together. Though our journey has not been easy and has had many ups and downs, Rick has remained my best friend, my husband, my partner. He supports my every dream.

Some days, I wonder how we are both standing with all the trials and tribulations we have seen over thirty-four years of marriage. There is no other heart as pure as his, and I have found in him the same qualities I admired in my dad. They are alike in many ways and maybe that's the reason l was attracted to him: his goodness. I can never thank him enough for all he's done for me as my life partner. Marriage is not always a bed of roses, but in our marriage, there has been fun, laughter, many wonderful surprises, and magic along with the struggles. I cannot think of a better person to share my life with. No, it's not always all magic and roses, but I can say the journey has been worth it.

And to think it all started with counting fishing tackle!

Chapter Twenty-One:
Guardian Angel

On a balmy summer night on the 18th of June in 1981, I was at home on summer vacation from college. I was 19, and had just finished my freshman year, and was relaxing in my parents' modest living room with the front door open.

A gentle breeze provided a cool comfort. A little over one month later, Princess Diana would wed Prince Charles, to put into perspective a happy and well-recalled event that was going on in the world during this time.

Some nights, I worried, late at night, about the safety of my street and neighborhood with good reason. Our neighborhood had been changing for years, and sadly continues to change to this day, and not in a good way.

Some summer nights, I would hear cars race down our small street and drivers screaming out their windows as they roared by. Our street was bordered by two fairly busy ones, and while these streets were not full-blown highways, they were pretty busy thoroughfares, one carrying people to and from the airport, and the other ran to another town in one direction and the heart of the inner city of Rochester, only about 3 or 4 miles away from us at most, in the other.

So, while I sat enjoying the late night, and television, and the warm summer weather, thoughts of my safety and my parents were never far from my mind. I always lived in a highly aware state of semi-anxiousness between years of being on "high alert" because of my addicted mother and the area we lived in. While not "rough," it was close enough to the city to warrant "caution."

Indeed, our house had been burglarized once when I was a child, and we were victims of smaller types of theft as well. My grandmother's house, just up the street, and my Aunt Frances's house had been burglarized as well. Consequently, all our homes had been fitted with security systems years before, as a precaution, and to give us some peace of mind. This happened at a time when most people of that era did not have them, at least not in smaller, modest homes like ours.

So, I sat that evening, relaxing, but always aware that anything could happen, I was aware that maybe I should get up and close and lock that front door. At about 10:30 the phone rang suddenly. I jumped.

Rrrrring! Rrrring!

"Hello, is your father home?" said a timid female voice, one I did not recognize.

"Um, yes, sure. Who's calling?"

"Linda Anderson. Amos Anderson's daughter."

"Hold on a minute. I'll go get him."

I walked into my dad's bedroom. "Dad!" I whispered as I gently shook him awake. "It's Amos Anderson's daughter on the phone for you!"

My dad bolted upright. He came out to the living room. After a couple of minutes, he set the phone down. He was white as a ghost. His friend, Amos Anderson, whom he had carpooled to his job at Xerox with, had been shot by his stepson and was in the hospital fighting for his life.

Earlier that day, 37-year-old William Bernard Griffin, Amos's stepson and an ex-Viet Nam veteran had murdered Amos' wife, who was Griffin's mother. Griffin shot Amos and killed Thomas Cariola, a painter, who had been in their house doing some work for the family.

Shortly after these shootings, Griffin flung his shotgun over his shoulder and calmly walked about a block or so to a nearby Security Trust bank, located on Thurston Road, in the City of Rochester. In broad daylight, on that beautiful summer afternoon, Griffin walked inside and took some of the tellers and customers hostage. He shot a 29-year-old bank teller and mother of two, Margaret Moore, killing her, then throwing the body with such force out of the front doors of the bank that it was nearly severed in half.

He also shot and wounded several others in the bank.

My family and I had watched on television hours earlier, and these events were broadcast on national television later that day.

Then the call came. Amos' daughter, looking for my dad.

Amos had told his daughter to contact my father to let him know he was still alive, and he was thinking of my dad. My dad always had that effect on people: When people were in trouble, sick, scared, had good news, or any kind of news, my dad was often the person, the friend, people wanted to call. He was a rock for everyone he knew.

The fact that Amos had his daughter call my dad on that terrible day solidified what I always knew in my heart about the kind of man my father was: kind, loving, caring, compassionate, understanding. Amos, in pain, and not knowing whether he would live or die, made the phone call, through his daughter to "Joe."

This fact was not lost on my dad, either, of how highly his friend regarded him, that even in pain and clinging to life, it was my father he wanted to get a message to, that he had survived. Though none of us spoke out loud or thought about the importance of that call, we just knew the gravity of Amos's injuries and what that call meant.

My dad had been inside that house, with Griffin, the shooter, just the day before, when he had dropped Amos off after work. I remember my father telling me how he had spoken briefly to Griffin, and talked to Amos's wife, who was dead not 24 hours later.

My dad expressed that nothing seemed out of the ordinary, but that Griffin was not at all friendly.

This infamous and tragic event has remained with me my whole life. Had my father been in that house just one day later, who knows what might have happened?

Griffin had threatened to continue his killing spree unless officers killed him. This scenario later came to be known as "Suicide by Cop." Once an officer from the SWAT team spotted Griffin in a bank window, he immediately shot and killed him. To this day, these events and the steps taken to react to a situation like this are used as a training scenario for police and SWAT teams.

I thank God my dad's name was not in "God's Book" that day, or for many days, weeks, months, and years to come. His Guardian Angel must have been with him during that period.

The echoes of that night are always with me, my vulnerability with that open front door and the calm, warm summer breezes that surrounded me and belied the day's earlier grisly violence and massacre not more than a few miles from our house.

God's protection was around me, our family, and especially my dad. He still had a lot of life left to live.

Chapter Twenty-Two: A Will to Live and God's Grace

I wanted to share that story with you before I told you this one.

We were at a family picnic. It was 1986, I was just 24 years old, and Rick and I had been married for only a year.

It was a hot July day. My father's face looked ashen and he had dark circles under his eyes. He seemed quieter and maybe a little on edge. As my husband and I left the picnic, I had a strange feeling in the pit of my stomach that I would later come to call "an echoey feeling."

I kissed Dad goodbye and watched him walk back through the cement parking lot, back towards the picnic grounds where all the family was still partying.

While walking to my car the weird feeling I was experiencing got worse. I've learned to identify that feeling better now and come to understand what it means. Every time I have had that feeling that I call "echoey" it is a premonition of either a near-death experience or an actual death. This feeling washes over me when I feel the angel of death nearby.

I hadn't had a lot of experience with the "echoey" feeling, yet, and didn't yet realize I would become more and more adept at recognizing it as years passed.

I don't remember much else, and I am not sure why. I couldn't remember if my mom called me the next day to tell me that my dad had had a heart attack either that night or the next morning. Only upon writing this, I remembered my dad made the call for the ambulance himself.

I remember him recounting, as he always did, everything that happened to him with humor. He told us how the ambulance workers rushed into the house, looked at him, and said: "Where is the patient?"

My dad, comically, and very slowly, as he was having crushing chest pain, slowly raised his hand in the air, as a student answering a question in class would have done.

When they realized he was the patient, he described comically how the "fur began to fly."

The EMTs were all amazed at his stoic and comical response to them and immediately began rushing around him, taking his vitals, giving oxygen, and peppering him with questions. Sure enough, my 60-year-old dad had a heart attack.

Dad had had a brother, Phil, who died when I was just 3 years old, at age 43 of a massive heart attack. His father had died of a heart attack suddenly, and he had a brother, Al, who died at age 56, in 1981, of what we initially thought was a heart attack, but later learned may have been an aortic aneurysm. So, his heart attack should have come as no surprise.

Only by the grace of God, and the evolution in medicine that meant open-heart surgeries were being performed and saving lives, my dad survived where others in his family had not.

My dad got sent home shortly after his heart attack and I don't remember visiting him in the hospital, although I am certain I must have. I also don't remember the ensuing month, where he was sent home, to recuperate from the heart attack before undergoing surgery.

I do recall him telling us, for the rest of his life, the agony he felt waiting an entire month to be strong enough for surgery. I recall him telling us how night after night he worried, staring up at the ceiling in his bedroom and praying. He became anxious, lying in his bed, waiting. He often spoke of thinking about how he might die before the month passed.

He didn't die. He went into surgery in August, a month after the heart attack. He explained how the doctor drew a picture of his heart, on a wrapper for a gauze dressing, which depicted how blocked several of his arteries were. He saved that "gauze picture" and I still have it, from when we cleaned out his house after he passed away.

I remember his entire extended family waiting at Rochester General Hospital for over seven hours. The surgery kept getting put off for one reason or another. By the time he went into the operating room the drugs they had given him to calm him down and partially sedate him, had worn off. I think they wheeled him into surgery somewhere around 2 p.m. In his words, he was wheeled in, wide awake, and seeing all the surgical apparatus, the respirator, and even the saws that would be used to cut his chest open.

And so, we waited, as the surgeons and God performed a miracle for us and Dad.

In August of 1986, he had a quintuple by-pass.

I remember feeling very scared and alone as we waited. To add to my anxiety, my husband had lost his job and was in another state for a job interview. Although I was surrounded by my mom and my aunts and my dad's sisters, I felt lonely. We all congregated in the front lobby area of the hospital.

I don't remember much else about that day except for when my mom and I were told we could go into the Intensive Care Unit. By this time, it was about 11 p.m. I had never seen anything like what I was about to see, and the image of my dad laying there is forever burned into my brain. Little did I know, I would repeat the horror of this sight, only ten times worse, 32 years later, when he underwent emergency brain surgery.

I walked in slowly, very scared of what I saw. He was alive, they told us. His body was so bloated I barely recognized him. Tubes were everywhere.

I think my mother called out to him: "Joe."

I also think I shushed her. She touched his hand, which did not even look like a hand but like a puffed-up stuffed sandbag. We were told later, he had about 16 extra pounds of fluid on his small frame due to the surgery, the trauma, and all the fluids and drugs they were giving him.

We both had tears in our eyes at the sight of him, and neither of us spoke. We were in shock. I remember a nurse walked over and told us that he would not be "out of the woods for at least 72 hours."

I don't remember much after that except that we stayed a while longer. We were only allowed in once for 15 minutes every two hours. We went home probably somewhere around 2 a.m.

I am not sure why I did not go to sleep at my mom's house to keep her company, but I am sure she told me to go home.

Dad returned home about a week later, and my mom nursed him slowly back to health. Little did we know, but years later, in 1995, Dad would return the favor of caring for her, after Mom also underwent open-heart surgery.

I never did get to thank his amazing surgeon, Dr. Jose Mijangos. Ironically, Dr. Mijangos, perished a few years later as did his partner, Dr. Fein, in a scuba diving accident in the Caribbean. I and my family always felt a deep debt of gratitude to this talented and compassionate heart surgeon.

About a year after my dad passed away, in 2018, I would run into his cardiologist, Dr. Theodore Stuver, whom my dad and family adore to this day. He marveled at the care my dad gave my mom after her surgery and through years of heart disease, even though he also struggled himself.

I will never forget the word he used to describe the care, love, and devotion my dad gave to my mom. "Meticulous," he said.

The story of his passing is for another time. As is the story of my mother and her passing.

Because no matter what else happened, above all my dad was simply, "Dad." He would be there for me and my mother through so many more things.

Chapter Twenty-Three: Someone, Call 9-1-1

Whether because of my life circumstance and the way I was brought up, or something else, panic attacks were a part of my own mental health struggle.

Did someone pull the chord to a lawnmower to jump-start my insides? I thought. Sitting rather calmly in a high school theology class, suddenly my heart went from what felt like "normal" to 6,000 beats per minute. All I knew was I needed to flee. I sat at my desk, heart pounding furiously, and prayed for this feeling to leave me. Too embarrassed to jump up and run, somehow the furious pounding in my chest subsided after many minutes.

What I did not know was this would be the first of many panic attacks I would have.

Truth be told, I had suffered and endured so much anxiety, home alone with my unstable mother, but I'd never experienced a random panic attack out of the blue. No saber-toothed tiger was chasing me. I was sitting in a classroom minding my own business.

A few years later, as a newlywed, my husband came home after I called him in a panic. He came to the little condo we moved into when we married and saw an ambulance there and me being carried out on a stretcher. He had lost his job that first year we were married, my dad had had a heart attack, and I was working in a stressful job as a stenographer at the New York State Attorney General's Office, working for a demanding and ruthless female attorney. I was at a breaking point.

It was another panic attack.

I thought I was having a heart attack. I remember being in our bedroom that morning and feeling a sense of doom wash over me. I also felt a sense of unreality. The next thing I knew, my heart was racing, and the more nervous and anxious I got, well, the more nervous and anxious I got. I called the ambulance.

Years prior, I had minor versions of these instances when under a lot of stress, but never full-blown panic attacks. I quit college at Nazareth, where I was enrolled in a speech-language pathology program and on the Dean's List, when, crazy as this may sound, I was in a clinical class in which we were going to have to be evaluated by our professor through a two-way mirror. This was the clinching point, the turning point for me. My husband-to-be begged me not to quit, but I did not listen.

Ironically, my quitting Nazareth, crying alone in my bedroom all summer long, and pondering what my next move would be would lead me to enroll at Bryant and Stratton College.

This is the nature of severe, pathological anxiety. It causes you to do things and make decisions you never would have under other circumstances. It truly derailed my life. I was always overly terrified of public speaking, of any attention on myself. I also can recall instances where, when I sought counseling for severe anxiety when first married, I became literally frozen and unable to speak.

I can recall a very torturous counseling appointment when I sought treatment for panic disorder (and later, agoraphobia—thankfully, I overcame both in a relatively short period). A psychiatrist sat face to face with me, and I am not sure if he thought I was being stubborn, insolent, rude or if he had insight into the terror in my heart, soul, and belly, and felt that just letting me writhe in discomfort would eventually help me see that the "tiger" wasn't real. This led us to a 45-minute staring contest, in which I wanted to crawl under the rug or flee the room. I did neither. My fear of even being in that situation was equivalent to being swallowed by a monster. I had a terror of even seeing a psychiatrist, for in my mind, I was becoming my mother. My voice and all my insides felt totally paralyzed. It was truly as if I could not speak. Is this what is known as "selective mutism?" It was a very frightening and gripping feeling.

I thought, *if I am here, I must be sick like her. And if doctors could not make her well in all these years, what will happen to me?*

Looking back, I have kicked myself a million and one times for quitting college, and for bailing out of many stressful situations. Literally, thousands of times, I had gone over the situation in my mind that I needed to quit. In hindsight, it was so benign and ridiculous, but at that time, the terror it provoked caused me to quit rather than face it. I have been angry at myself for years for this awful mistake that truly changed the course of my life. But when someone suffers debilitating anxiety and possesses untreated trauma, no amount of talking or rationalization can convince them that the tiger will not consume them whole. In my case, the "tiger" was public speaking, feeling "all eyes" on me.

This kind of anxiety truly is an illness, and few understand it; even fewer get the treatment they need so they can succeed in their lives. What's heartbreaking to me is that it is not a lack of intelligence or desire or persistence, but a true mental illness, that when not properly addressed can have lifelong consequences, as it did for me. It caused me to give up and not pursue a career I most likely would have enjoyed and flourished in. As life went on, I settled. I worked in low-level jobs. After some years, I had my wonderful children, whom I adore, and threw myself into being the best mom I could be. I wanted nothing more than to give them the home life I often did not have. Years after that, my focus and our finances went into trying to give my girls the education that I never finished, and I also later became a caretaker to all my family.

IT WAS ALWAYS YOU AND ME

No amount of trying to describe how my anxiety has unfortunately shaped and defined my life can do it justice here in a few short paragraphs, but, paradoxically, it has led me to what many people do: Living Plan B for my life and trying to make it the best I possibly could, and to the story I am telling now.

I feel I must tell people my story now. This was my destiny: to tell the story I have actually lived. Counseling through the years, age, maturity, life experiences have all finally given me my voice, even if my voice has come to me later in life.

My voice was always within me; it was always there, but writing too, is my best means of self-expression and my attempt to help others who struggle with anxiety and in finding themselves and perhaps finding a voice they feel was silenced. Mine was silenced due to the era I grew up in, and my very private family who needed to keep my mother's illness a secret. I was complicit with their strict instructions and the spoken and unspoken rules of conduct I was expected to guard at all costs.

Silence and secrets, however, breed nothing good.

My mother's illness had severe repercussions on my psyche as, most likely, did early abandonment as an infant, before my adoption. While I could not control either of these events or the events, I have suffered due to my mother's horrific addiction, and the subsequent abuse and neglect I often suffered growing up, it is truly my wish and my hope that my story will give people hope that you can persist, you can succeed

and you can find yourself and your voice eventually,
as I have. Others in my family were not so fortunate.

Chapter Twenty-Four:
Waiting for the Other Shoe to Drop

Maybe it's an odd place to start I'm not sure. Visions of that threadbare non-descript wool (was it wool?) taupe-brownish-greyish fibers making up Aunt Frances' worn-out carpet will stay forever in my mind.

The house itself smelled like her bobby pins if bobby pins could have a smell. Aqua Net® hairspray, cigarette smoke, and endless pitchers of minted iced tea created the sensory cocktail that greeted me. That and deep sadness, emptiness, and her feelings of desperation and hopelessness clinging to every room.

The one small silver of hope was the candy drawer she always kept for me. I was the daughter she never had, she told me. Despite the deep depression she couldn't shake, she always smiled and laughed with me, prayed with me, and encouraged me.

The cupboards were always mostly bare. She had no money.

The pleather yellowish-vanilla-ish recliner, the blond wood furniture that even in the 1970s was probably twenty-years out of date, and of course, the little plastic Magnum organ that sat off to the side were things I would often remember when I dreamed of this room.

In the absence of the ability to help her, my childish mind thought: "If only I could buy some of the things, she needs to fix up that sparse house. If I could eradicate some of the poverty and fill things up and make them beautiful for her, would that save her?"

She was my mom's identical twin. Twice divorced. Her second husband was a fly-by-night, get-rich-quick, scheming, con-artist type. I'm told had a very brilliant mind but had a few bats in the attic. He mistreated her, didn't pay bills, and they fought all the time. He gambled and cheated on her, and when he lost his bowling alley business to some shrewd Jewish businessmen, the last of his marbles went with it.

Strike three, nothing to spare.

They fought, and he didn't even come to the hospital when she had over seven major abdominal surgeries. When he finally did show up, after she laid there in bed with a colostomy, he tried to convince her she had cancer.

She didn't. Then my family had to convince her she didn't. Was he crazy or evil or both? No one knew, but he just up and left her and her nine-year-old son. Thankfully, her parents, (my grandparents) tried their best to help and pick up the pieces, along with my mother, my dad, and her other sister, Millie, and my Uncle Tom.

Once, I remembered to ask if she had a wedding ring. She said she did, but when he didn't pay the bills, she sold it to pay her taxes.

After a couple of attempts at suicide, one of which brought her home with actual brain damage, when the drapes were drawn and she didn't answer her phone, we worried.

I was at home crying in my room and frightened of what would become of her.

Eventually, some healing came. But we were always on guard. Always waiting for the other shoe to drop. Always scared for her.

In my condo, newly married, a call came on a Monday evening. "Please come home, it's your aunt."

I cried. A close friend came over and I remember she bent down and tied my shoes for me because I was so distraught not knowing what happened to my beloved aunt. We drove to my parents' home.

First, I saw my cousin, her son. He hugged me. I cried some more. No one said much.

Later, I found out that my dad found her. In the "little room" as she called her sparsely decorated den. I was 27. She was 63. My beloved aunt was dead from an apparent suicide.

We didn't tell my grandmother. It was 3 or 4 days before Thanksgiving. I marveled at my family's resilience.

"Cook the turkey," my Aunt Millie said. "We still have to eat."

Chapter Twenty-Five: The Stork and Chicken Soup

Only a couple of years later, it must have been in May of 1991, when I passed the test. The pregnancy test, that is. I stood there, staring at the little stick, my eyes and brain not completely registering the pink line, which meant "positive."

It's not that Rick and I had been "trying," but it wasn't like we had been "not trying" either. In fact, I don't remember any "trying" at all.

I walked, zombie-like, out to the backyard where Rick was mowing the lawn. I said nothing, just unceremoniously handed him the pink stick. He smiled and hugged me.

In truth, it was not a matter of not being happy, but we were scared. We were going to be parents!

I told my mother I was pregnant shortly after, on the phone. I always had this innate shyness about me. You see, even though I'd been married for 6 years, and 29 years old, I still felt my family didn't approve of sex or, at least, anything related to me and that subject. I mean, I knew they always wanted grandkids. How was

I supposed to produce grandchildren for them without having sex? Well, that was another story. Possibly they hoped for an immaculate conception? Or so I felt.

So, I told my mother, and she told my dad. I wondered how I would face him. I mean, now he would KNOW I had had sex. As if he didn't already? Yes, I realized this, but still, I felt the irrational fear of their opinion of me actually doing the deed. Ridiculous, right?

Well, I faced my parents and the world. Yes, I had been married for 6 years, and the world knew: I had sex and I was pregnant. Oh my God. I must have been the first woman ever that this happened to.

But all was well! Everyone was happy, especially Rick and me. My mother made sure to remind me daily that she was amazed that I had no morning sickness.

Then it hit. Week six. The vomiting began and, wheeling me in 9 months later for my C-section, the doctor remarked, "Give her something. We cannot have her heaving while we're cutting her open."

Welcome to pregnancy. Glorious it was not. This was just post-Olivia-Newton John era, the "Let's Get Physical" era of watching cute preggos in their workout clothes, having gained only the requisite 20 pounds expected on the television. I watched these types, gorgeous, with tiny figures and color-coordinated outfits, sweatbands adorning their heads as they exercised, Jazzercised, and aerobicized their way through pregnancies. They were always stylish, barely breaking a sweat and extolling the virtues of pregnancy all while showing off just the cutest little pregnancy "bump." To say I felt cheated and was envious of those types would be a grotesque understatement.

Once the vomiting began, it was so vicious I could barely shower. I would have to step out midway through, puke, and then finish. The nausea began every single morning before I was quite awake. It was so bad, I kept a pan of sorts at the foot of my bed because I would wake up and throw up, not even able to make it to the bathroom.

I tried every home remedy; read everything I could get my hands on. I only got very mild relief from any of the recommendations. There was an entity, a being, growing inside, spinning in utero, and my head and guts were spinning daily, too. I wore sea-sickness bands, I had to eat solid food and drink liquid separately. I tried a medicine, after the first trimester, briefly, and maybe on only two occasions, that just made me sleepy, but still, I threw up.

So, it was difficult, to say the least, to get excited over the impending baby, when all I did was throw up day and night. To distract myself, I tried to keep on working at the law firm where I was employed. Although I worked fewer hours for the first couple of months, the attorneys accommodated me.

I planned a garage sale, I was busy getting the baby's room ready, trying to distract myself by picking out furniture and wallpaper, and unbelievably in my sixth month of pregnancy, Rick and I even planned a trip and flew to Las Vegas to visit my cousins, where I threw up every day as well, but at least I was distracted.

My Grandma Angelina was still living, and now that the issue of the "white veil" was obviously moot, she threw herself into damage control, which consisted of her making me one of the only things I could keep down: large vats of her homemade chicken soup. My grandmother was now 87 years old, and she made me soup every week. My pregnancy, like everything else in my life, was a family mission. My dad would fetch me, most weekdays on my lunch hour, from the law firm I was working and puking at downtown and bring me to his house where he and my mom would load me up with Grandma Baldo's chicken soup. About a half-hour to forty-five minutes into my lunch hour, my dad would say: "Ok, I better get you back to work!" With my stomach somewhat settled, still exhausted but a bit better, I returned to work. The nausea never completely left.

My mom was uncharacteristically tough with me during this time, saying things like: "Well, you bought that house, and what else are you going to do?" Translated meant, as I knew: "Go back to work, you need the money!"

Everything was always spinning. I could only think about this little universe, spinning inside of me, growing. All that motion made me nauseous. But, in truth, I always had this vague awareness of the world spinning around and outside of me.

I wondered about the possibility of other 'universes,' other realities. Other people's lives were surely evolving and spinning, and simultaneously other lives were happening. Other things, things beyond my wildest imagination were happening "out there" unbeknownst to me. Now it was the baby, its cells growing and spinning, dividing, and becoming.

The fact that I could sense these "things" wouldn't be revealed to me for, at least, a couple more decades, not in a way I could understand. But they were real, for sure. They had happened and would be revealed to me most shockingly. They would come to me in the form of siblings I never dreamed I had, out in the universe, living their reality. But for now, I had my world. My baby was coming.

Months passed, and after a tortuously long labor followed by an unplanned cesarean section our beautiful Shannon Renee was born in January of 1992.

She was and is, the light of our family; my parents became first-time grandparents and were over the moon.

We didn't really try to have a second child, any more than we tried to have the first one.

My dad with one of his granddaughters—my oldest daughter, Shannon, at about age 2. The kids were always the "loves of his life." His expression says it all.

I think my husband "hung his pants up" and I was pregnant.

Our older daughter was three, I was thirty-three, so the timing was right if we were going to have another child.

The morning sickness wasn't quite as severe as the first time around, but it was still there in a full-time capacity, unrelenting and merciless.

My mother was too sick to come to the ultrasound, the one where we would find out what gender baby we would be having. My husband and dad came in her place, and when the doctor told us we were having a girl, we were thrilled.

Just before or just after the ultrasound, my mother underwent open-heart surgery, the same surgery my dad had when he was sixty after having a heart attack. The need for hers was a botched angiogram.

Her blood vessels were so brittle from years of high blood pressure and smoking that when they attempted to put the catheter for the procedure into her artery, it ripped, and she suffered a heart attack on the operating table.

The surgeon performed emergency open-heart surgery right away.

Of course, I got a call that something had gone wrong, and I should come to the hospital right away. Rick, my three-year-old daughter and, of course, my pregnant belly raced to the hospital, only to end up waiting for hours before the surgeon came out with the simple announcement:

"I think she'll make it."

The rest of my pregnancy was accompanied by my mother's grueling recovery and the start of her battle with heart failure.

This time we "scheduled" the birth of our daughter via c-section on March 14. My daughter Shannon had a school field trip, so my Aunt Millie accompanied her while we went to the hospital. She and her husband, Tom, planned to bring her to see me and her new sister right after that.

Jaimee Ann, my second daughter, was born on March 14, 1996. She had strawberry blonde hair and the bluest of eyes.

One of my favorite pictures of my girls.

She was also my youngest daughter, and my mother announced that she and Rick could not handle any more morning sickness if I got pregnant again. So, she declared that, if they did not tie my tubes during the C-section, she and Rick would come into the operating room and assist the surgeon by doing it themselves.

My grandmother, my aunt and uncle, my daughter, my husband, and my in-laws were all there to welcome the new addition to our family.

We brought her home two days later. I was upset that there was no big stork sign in the yard as most people did those days (somehow that important detail had gotten overlooked this time) but was no indication of any absence of our overwhelming joy. These details were important, and we had not made a proper yard-announcement.

The family was overjoyed, and our two daughters are still the light of our lives. I remember my dad saying, "If I could lasso the moon and give it to my granddaughters, I would."

Our family was complete.

Me and my two babes.

Part Three

If I could sit across the porch from God,

I'd thank Him for lending me, You.

— Elle Cosimance

Chapter Twenty-Six: Rescue Me

I, Diane, have spent the better part of my life simultaneously rescuing myself, and yet feeling as though I needed to be rescued.

I know I am not alone in this, and although it may sound confusing to someone who has not had the same experience, it is true. I was forced to stay afloat and be self-sufficient to survive my mother's illness, and I became resilient in the face of her damaging verbal abuse.

I know she did not seek deliberately to hurt me. As has been said, your parents did the best they could at the time, but their actions may have hurt you and shaped you anyway. That was especially true with my mother.

This pain has affected me in multiple ways. I am slow to trust, suffer from anxiety and phobias, and even low self-esteem.

Yet, I am a warrior. I fought despite these hindrances, and despite obstacles I had to overcome, I have accomplished great things. I married, raised a family, and have become a lifelong learner, pursuing a degree "late" in life. I want to improve myself and do more than just survive, but to thrive.

My mother's illness, you understand, affected everyone around her and her relationships. Her actions contradicted what she expected of me. She did not make good choices when it came to her mental health and the pills she was addicted to. I shared here about my mother and her illness, and how it affected me and my dad and our relationship.

But I was expected to do better, and not to take pills or smoke cigarettes or be self-destructive in any way. Instead, I was expected to work hard, become independent, get an education, and to do better for myself and my family, and I did.

That does not mean I do not struggle. I suffer from paranoia, obsess over other peoples' reactions even as I write this book. These things flow out of the abuse I suffered at her hands.

There are times when I have needed help, rescue if you will. My dad, my Aunt Millie, Uncle Tom, Grandma Baldo, Aunt Frances, my cousin Tony, and his wife, Jane, and friends and neighbors, only a few of whom are mentioned in this book, all have played that role at one time or another with me.

I've recounted here how my mom's anger when I was young would leave me terrified, bewildered, and confused. As a young child, I often felt she hated me and would try to poison me. My mind came up with that crazy idea somehow due to the intense meanness and anger she showed towards me when she was taking pills, even though the more rational side of me, even as a child could not really believe she would ever do anything to harm me.

I never knew what might come next, and I often sought to escape. I would try to predict her episodes to be one step ahead of them, and actually became quite good at it. I developed a "sixth sense" when it came to my mother. I felt I had to in order to survive her wild mood swings and aggressive behavior towards me while she was "under the influence." Crazy as it may sound there was a certain "predictability" in her unpredictability and I became an expert, whether I wanted to or not, in learning her patterns. As I have mentioned before, although I was adopted, I felt she and I had an attachment even closer than if we were biologically related and oddly her addiction was one reason I became so mentally and emotionally attuned to her. As an adult, anxiety and depression came as I was always waiting for the other shoe to drop. I was constantly on guard and hypervigilant, an exhausting state.

As a result, I developed panic attacks starting in high school, but worsening in my twenties. For a time, I didn't want to eat in restaurants for fear of being poisoned. It sounds crazy, but to me, I thought if my mother would try to hurt me, why wouldn't a total stranger try to harm me too? After all, there are a lot of crazy people in the world.

I could not help how I felt. It took a few years along with the loving patience of my husband to get over them. I felt embarrassed, odd, and alone, unable to even to share them with anyone.

But as I became an adult, I learned there were others like me, who grew up in dysfunctional families where drug addiction and alcoholism existed, and they were as familiar as siblings. Some did have the love of extended family, relatives, and neighbors to help them cope and become resilient like I did.

I have always felt deficient in some areas like math and mechanics. I know little about sports, am directionally challenged and often joke I have little of the "typically male abilities and traits." But I am creative and affectionate and have discovered other ways to express myself. I tried, despite her illness and resulting abuse, to be a good daughter and friend to my mother.

Mom and Dad, May 7, 1991,
at their 45th wedding anniversary party.

I love to connect with new people, make new friends, and share my thoughts, feelings, and ideas. I love to cook, bake, and entertain friends and family, all things that are part of my nurturing side. I want to help those around me.

And I love humor, and I credit a lot of that to my family. No matter how bad things got, my dad, and even my mom, when well, always instilled and underscored the importance of humor in surviving whatever life throws at us.

In the end, God gave me many rescuers to help me navigate the toughest parts of my life. Their loving support gave me examples that showed me how to rescue myself. Their role as blessings in my life revealed my ability to survive. We are all so much stronger than we believe ourselves to be.

Why do I tell you these things now? Because I want to tell you a little more about my Aunt Millie.

She was one of those rescuers, and I have fond memories of my time with her, from the time I stayed with her as a child until she passed.

I'll let those stories speak for themselves.

Chapter Twenty-Seven: Cake Batter

Helpless. That's how we felt.

I would sit, sobbing, heart pounding, thin arms sticking to the plastic tablecloth that covered by aunt and uncle's dining table. My Aunt Millie sat at one end, sadness in her eyes.

My Uncle Tom occasionally would come to the table and sit, but rarely spoke. He was just there, sitting and watching.

I felt small, embarrassed, and shamed. Always shamed. My mother's illness was not my fault, but it was my burden anyway.

"Honey, don't worry," my aunt would say. From time to time, she would try to get a laugh out of me with an exclamation: "That bastard."

I tried to smile, but most of the time I simply felt like my heart would explode. I felt like an old woman at the young age of twelve or thirteen.

We would sit at her kitchen table for hours, not knowing what to do, none of us knowing what to say. Not one of us. They loved me, I knew it, but we were all drowning in the waves of pain my mother set in motion.

I couldn't swim. Helpless. We were all helpless.

And this was not a one-time event. It went on for years. When I stayed with them, as night fell, I would go to sleep in a little twin bed set up in my aunt's sewing room. My uncle would go to bed, quiet and solemn.

If I did not go to bed right away, my aunt and I would retreat to the living room from the kitchen. We would talk more, and she would make me a snack or some hot chocolate.

Those moments are some of the best times of my life, nestled among the moments that were the worst.

Their home was the escape from the craziness at my house. My mother was not killing her sadness, anger, disappointment, or even the pain she experienced. Instead, she was ruining her health and damaging all of those around her who cared: my dad, me, her twin sister Frances, Aunt Millie, Uncle Tom, and my grandmother.

We had more practical things to consider than my mother's illness though.

How long could I stay? How long would it take for this to end?

How could my aunt get more clothes for me? She didn't want to go over to my house any more than I did.

Would the school bus change its route to pick me up?

Should she take my mom to court, and find out if I could live with them permanently?

Could she talk to my mom's psychiatrist and find out what was going on with her, and what could be done about it?

I remember her trying to do just that one time. I sat on one of those little leather-covered stools by a telephone nook in the kitchen. I could hear both ends of the conversation.

"Hello, this is Mildred Maggio, my sister is Ann DiProspero, she is a patient of Dr. Canapary's," my aunt said.

"Yes, Mrs. Maggio, how can we help you?"

"Well, I would like to talk to Dr. Canapary. My sister is a very sick woman. She has been coming to him for many years now. She is not getting well, in fact, she's getting worse. We are all worried about her and her daughter, too."

"Mrs. Maggio, I am very sorry, but these are confidential matters. The doctor can't speak to you about your sister."

Slowly, my aunt hung up. She looked like she was about to scream, and then like she might cry.

"Aunt Mill, what did they say?" I asked.

"Honey, I am sorry. That bastard is a quack! They won't talk to me," she said. "Oh, God, I don't know what to do!"

"It's okay, Aunt Mill," was all I could manage.

I don't remember how advanced or what antidepressant medication was even available in those days, what types or kinds of counseling, or what other help my mother could get. Who would expect me to? I was just a kid.

What I did know was that my mother complained of vicious, unrelenting headaches, and this is what she was supposedly medicating herself for. She had severe hypertension and depression as well, I am sure, although no one spoke of that. Perhaps even the high blood pressure was the source of the headaches.

But no one knew. It was as if her true diagnosis and how to treat it, were both mysteries that remained unanswered.

So, I would stay at my aunt's for days and weeks at a time. My aunt would sometimes muster the courage to go to my house when my dad was there and grab some items of mine. It was like navigating a minefield. She never knew my mother's mood or what she might walk into. My mother could be vicious, wildly screaming out of her head, or behaving in other crazy ways.

My dad would try to mitigate the screaming while my aunt ran to my bedroom to gather some of my belongings to take back to her house.

Eventually, over days or weeks, the storm would calm. My dad would come to my aunt's begging me to go home. I didn't want to. I was happy at my aunt's where at least I had some peace.

Through all the chaos, I would still have schoolwork to do and keep a stiff upper lip during the day at school because, God forbid, anyone should know what was going on at my house. That would only add to my shame and the fear that my life would somehow implode, and not in a good way if anyone found out. I was sworn to secrecy from a young age, and this burden weighed heavily on my heart. I rarely smiled during those days.

Life would go on. I would stay with Aunt Millie and Uncle Tom during the frequent storms. I felt safe there. On weekends it was so nice—on Friday and sometimes Saturday nights, my uncle would be off bartending and so would my dad. My uncle in those days worked at the Mapledale Party House, where he was the bar manager. The Mapledale was an iconic Rochester venue of sorts, hosting thousands of weddings, banquets, corporate events and more. My dad at this point was bartending at another well-known venue, simply known as "The Party House," that also hosted the same type of events, and where my dad earned a reputation, as did my uncle, of really professional bartenders, my dad being known locally by hundreds as "Little Joe" (of the "Party House").

Aunt Millie and Uncle Tom at "The Party House," where my dad bartended, his second job for over 25 years. This photo was taken at a surprise 45th wedding anniversary party that we had for my parents. Mom always felt bad that, since she "eloped" in 1945, she never really had a wedding with family and friends. This party was my attempt to give her and Dad the wedding they never had.

Dad at his surprise 90ᵗʰ birthday party at a local party house in Rochester. That cake was made to look like a "golf course," because he so loved to golf!

My sick mother was home alone, dealing with her issues, and I was with my aunt avoiding them. We would go out to eat together or cook at her house. Lots of times we went shopping at our local Long Ridge and Greece Towne Mall, and then always out for hot fudge sundaes afterward.

Back home, we would watch all kinds of shows on television that were popular: *The Bob Newhart Show, The Mary Tyler Moore Show, The Carol Burnett Show,* and others.

My aunt sat across from me in one of the two beige colored recliners that were hers and my uncle's, and I sat in one of the two armchairs separated by a beautiful round marble-topped end table with a large lamp. There we sat, laughing at the television.

My heart, though heavy for a kid, could forget for, at least, a little while. I know my aunt was under tremendous stress, but she never let on. She was lighthearted, always smiling and laughing, my angel.

Sundays would roll around.

"Honey, did you sleep okay in the spare room?" she would ask.

"Yeah, I slept okay," I would lie. The bed wasn't very comfortable, and after she would go join my uncle in their bedroom, I would spend most school nights and weekend nights crying into my pillow for hours.

On Sunday mornings, when life was normal and I was at home, there were church services with my dad. I sang in a children's folk choir. But when I was staying at my aunt's we did not go to church on Sunday mornings.

"Diane, get dressed," said Aunt Millie one Sunday.

"Okay," I replied.

"C'mon, sweetheart, we are baking a cake!"

Out came the Sunbeam® mixer and we would start. In the milky colored bowl, I could see my wan expression, my big black eyes, blackened by crying night after night, and my silky black hair. I didn't look healthy. I looked sunken, depressed, thin, and not at all like a child, but like a worn-out adult. I felt weak and tired from sorrow.

But as we mixed and poured the batter, sometimes thick yellow and sometimes chocolate batter, adding our flavorings, we experimented with recipes, flavors, and textures. As the beaters whizzed, my heart slowed. I was transported, I guess today people would say I was in the flow. I was lost in our baking, and I could hear my aunt's voice, but my mind was a million miles away.

I would stare into the bowl and be transported, into the cake batter. I felt calm.

"What flavor should we put in there today?" she would ask.

"I don't know," I would reply, half not caring, half trying to hide my sadness. I was unable to muster any enthusiasm but then kicked myself mentally, knowing full well my aunt was trying her hardest to be upbeat, to distract me, and to make life more pleasant.

I could not rise to the challenge a lot of the time, and then felt sad and guilty for that as well. The burden was too heavy. I was a kid and couldn't save my mother. None of us could.

Shouldn't I be able to save her? Why couldn't I?

Somehow the trance would be broken. I'd find myself in one of my aunt's homemade aprons, and she would persist.

"Do you think we should throw a little rum flavoring in there?" She would look at me to see if I caught that throwing a little "rum" in there was a naughty thing to do. She would wink and try to see my reaction.

This would get me to smile.

"Sure, Aunt Mill! That's a great idea," I would say, and we both would laugh.

"No one will know," she would say, putting a finger over her lips as if to say, "It's our secret."

"Should we throw a little whiskey in the batter, too?" she would ask.

Then she would say: "It's okay with me darlin'. You do what you want!"

I cannot remember if we did or not. But I knew that it was all okay when I was with Aunt Mill. She was sweet, and kind, and loved me so very much. She was mischievous and our problems swirled and swirled in that cake batter. We mixed and baked, cried, laughed, and prayed.

My mother never really did get well, not until after my children were born, but by then her health was very bad from all the abuse her body had taken.

She did manage to be a wonderful grandmother. Despite all the hell we all went through, I knew she tried to be a good mother, too, although she was unable to at the time.

It was those times, thankfully, my aunt, uncle, my mom's twin sister, and my grandmother picked up the slack and raised me when they could. When they could not, I often was home alone in my bedroom, while my dad was away bartending, moonlighting to make ends meet.

During those times, I had to raise myself, rescue myself, if you will. I often had to shut my bedroom door and seal myself away from my mother's screaming and ranting. I'm not sure who protected me then. God? My inner willpower and strength?

But every Sunday morning, when my mom would gather herself together enough for me to return home, I would go back to church with my dad and sing in the choir.

Afterward, I went to Aunt Millie's where we baked our cakes, always different, always experimenting, always breaking the rules, and rebelling against what the recipes for cake or life told us to do. Every Sunday, I lost myself in the swirling cake batter.

My aunt lovingly remained in the background trying to rescue my broken heart, to save me, one Sunday, one cake at a time. I still can see and hear her excitement, her love, and I still drift off when baking into the luscious batter, whirling and swirling in the milky colored bowl, promising me relief and escape, mesmerizing me like a cake sea. Almost like meditating, as I watched all the ingredients blend, I wished my sadness could be mixed and blended and just disappear. Staring hypnotically, it was healing to my mind to go to another place where I could escape the madness, if only for a little while.

My Aunt Millie remained a rock to me, even as I grew into adulthood, and it was my turn to take care of her and her husband.

Chapter Twenty-Eight: Naked After 90

As Aunt Millie and Uncle Tom got older, Rick and I helped take care of them, and his sister Patty sometimes helped us, as she worked as a home health aide. Sometime in 2012, Patty called Rick one morning.

"I can't get in the house," she said. "The screen door is locked."

Now, we'd told Aunt Millie not to lock the back screen door so Patty could get into the house, but she often "forgot." She was well into her diagnosis with Alzheimer's at this point, so changing her lifelong habits was difficult to say the least.

Also, by this time, my Uncle Tom, while lucid, had Meniere's disease, which wreaked havoc with his equilibrium because of its effect on his inner ear.

You would think they would have one of those cool little call buttons, the ones you wear around your neck and can summon help with if something happens, right?

They did, or, at least, Aunt Millie did. On this particular morning, it was probably tucked away on her nightstand on a jewelry hanger. She didn't even wear it anymore, nor would she have necessarily remembered what to do with it.

Both were stone deaf. My aunt's hearing was a little better than my uncle's, but her comprehension was exponentially worse.

Anyway, while my sister-in-law, Patty, waited for us, she peered in the front picture window to see if she could get the attention of either of them.

Not only was Aunt Millie not wearing her "I've fallen, and I can't get up" necklace, but she also was not wearing anything at all.

And she was on top of my nearly naked Uncle Tom.

Patty chuckled at first, but then that humor turned to alarm. She called Rick who called me, and we rushed over.

Rick managed to break in the back screen door and get inside to get the pair upright and dressed.

Apparently, my uncle fell, and my aunt, 85 pounds at her heaviest, tried to pick him up, but due to her frail condition, that wasn't possible.

They didn't normally run around their house in the buff, but since it was early, my aunt had been washing up for the day, heard the fall, and rushed out to "help."

The rest, as they say, is history.

We then bought them matching terrycloth wrap-around towels, the kind you Velcro around your body at the top, and they comically posed in them a couple days later, each wearing a huge grin. Well, and the rest of their clothes.

Rick and I became expert at dealing with these mishaps and shenanigans over the long process of caring for them.

This was far from the only incident. Another time, dressed, but sans hearing aids, my aunt walked to the back of her walk-in closet at her home.

My Uncle Tom could not find her. He kept calling out for her, but, of course, she heard nothing. So, convinced that she had wandered off and left the house to go shopping or something, something she was notorious for doing, he got in his car.

Being 95 himself, he still drove all over town, searching the routes to various stores like Walmart, the Dollar store, and other places she might go.

He searched and searched but found no Aunt Millie.

In a panic, he called my dad with the news that Millie had gone missing. My dad, close to 90 himself, jumped in his car and drove around searching for my uncle.

Who was searching for my aunt?

He called Rick and me.

Rick jumped in the car, and in a "woman who swallowed a spider to catch the fly" comedy, now Rick was looking for my dad, who was looking for my uncle, who was looking for my aunt.

Of the pursuers, I'm not sure who circled back around to the homestead first to see if perhaps wayward Aunt Millie had returned, but that person discovered Millie, calm and cool as a cucumber, sitting in her recliner watching television.

And as they say, "That's when the fight started."

She insisted she had been home the whole time. My Uncle Tom insisted she had been nowhere to be found.

We (and they) were truly blessed that no one was hurt during these crazy episodes. God must have been watching over the pair, who were married for an amazing 73 years.

She always knew who we were, remained cheerful and never got combative as some other dementia patients do, and only became a bit ornery at the very end of her life when we put her in an assisted living facility.

This tale is also not told to mock my amazing family. We all deal with such things as we care for our elders, and often laughter was the key to survival and your mental health even when things get their toughest.

And when my aunt neared the end, things admittedly got tougher.

Chapter Twenty-Nine: A Soul in the City

In 2015, Aunt Millie was diagnosed with Lewy body dementia. That is when the shit hit the fan, so to speak.

For the last three years of her life, we watched her slip away. The woman, once filled with boundless energy, the family matriarch, cook, seamstress, my best friend, and confidant, started to deteriorate.

Once a great baker, she poured powdered brownie mix into a bowl, set it in front of my 18 and 21-year-old daughters, and declared, "There ya' go!"

Their tear-filled eyes said it all. Now we were caring for the woman who had cared for us.

"We can't eat these like this," one of the girls told her. "We need to mix them up and cook them first."

But she just looked at them. "Oh," she said and smiled.

Welcome to the world of someone with Alzheimer's.

My official role as a caretaker, although it had started when I was a young child in many ways, began when I was pregnant with my daughter Jaimee and my mother got sick. She passed away in 2003, a victim of deterioration caused by years of abusing her own body.

Twelve years later, I found myself helping plan my oldest daughter's wedding, a huge Italian affair, working, and sitting in hospice with Aunt Millie.

She'd always been shy of 100 pounds, the seamstress, who on Sundays after the big dinner at her house, would sit as we modeled our latest clothes, my daughters often in school uniforms.

She would get on her hands and knees with an old-fashioned measuring stick, chalk, and pins filling her mouth, telling us over and over:

"Turn. Turn. Turn."

My Uncle Tom would grumble about all the wayward pins all over the floor.

Now she lay in bed, on hospice, quite literally starving, and there wasn't a thing any of us could do about it. Down to a mere 74 pounds, eyes transfixed and glossy, she appeared almost corpse-like. Her breath came in shallow gasps but remained steady and constant. Her cheeks were hollow, and she seemed to hover between the earth and some far-off place we could not see.

"Be strong," I told myself, but the pain in my heart would not let me be.

We would have been terrified had we not known what was coming. Instead, we took turns, holding a bedside vigil, each one of us praying death would come and deliver her from this suspended and grotesque state. She deserved a better kind of death.

In life, she was reserved, private, funny, innocent, cheerful, and generous. Why would God allow her to continue like this?

All we could do was watch, and our helplessness made us feel somehow responsible. With nothing to do but observe someone we loved so fiercely die slowly in front of our eyes, we were moved to protest, to do something when there was nothing to be done.

My dad, now a widower of a dozen years and nearly 90 himself, sat faithfully with us every day.

Her caretakers could not give her any more morphine. She was receiving the most they could give. She never wanted this kind of death: long and drawn out, yet here she was, and here we were.

"Mr. DiProspero," the caretakers would say, concerned. "Why don't you go home and get some rest?"

"Oh, no," he would reply. "I'll stay."

He was not about to leave Millie alone, and neither was I. He would eat by her bedside, his beloved Yankees on the television.

My mind wandered. Was there nothing we could do? Could we not pull her back from the brink of death and hold onto her a little while longer?

My heart was torn from me. Surely, she would never have allowed me to suffer in this state. We shoot animals who are in pain to put them out of their misery, yet we let our loved ones die grueling deaths.

The hospice workers tried to placate us, telling us she was comfortable. She did not look comfortable, lying motionless in a hospital bed, mouth open but taking in no food or liquids for days. Our family watched as she slipped away, Alzheimer's taking her, winning the battle, and showing us who was boss.

Certainly, it was not us mere mortals.

My oldest daughter's wedding was days away. Her joy was overshadowed by the interminable waiting. It seemed horrible of us to wish for her death, but there was no comfort in anything else, and we understood there was no hope.

The entire place, the hospice facility, took on an otherworldly aura. Everything smelled of death, no matter how hard we tried to think of this place as one of welcome, comfort, mercy, or any other adjective. It reeked of the end, and the smell made me sick.

I would flee outside from time to time for a breath of fresh air. My chest felt like it would explode under the weight of my grief. I could not call my mother, as she was already gone. I would not call or cry out to my uncle: he was in assisted living himself, 95 years old, and my aunt's impending death had put him into a hazy state of half-consciousness as his mind tried to protect him from the devastating but inevitable loss ahead.

When he visited her, he moaned and cried and mumbled over her bedside, often unaware of who she was, thinking she was his mother, sister, or someone else. It wasn't dementia but simply shock. We worried he might never return to his right mind.

I would pace the sidewalk, alone. I would rub my chest, trying to prevent what I was sure was a coming heart attack. I would cry tears by the bucketful. No help came, no relief came. I was on my own.

One day, a good friend of mine named Jill came to visit and I felt like an angel had arrived.

She stayed, and prayed with me and my aunt, comforting us the best she could.

My cousins came, too, and my best friend, Michelle. They were godsends to me, just the comfort I needed.

I would run by there every day, on my lunch hour, after work, weekends, whenever I could. My husband was there when he could be. Rick could not stay long and just stare at her. It was too hard for him.

My kids came in and out too when they were able. But they were living. Millie was dying, and they could do nothing to help her. Seeing her that way was tearing their hearts out as well.

And I was there, for all intents and purposes facing this alone, as I had done with my mother and her death years before. I would do this again, with all my family who passed on. I would watch them deteriorate, plan their funerals, take care of their business and homes when they were gone, and bury them one by one.

They all passed away within two and a half years of each other. I'm not sure how I survived that time, except to say that the enormity of their personalities, their goodness and love, and all they had instilled in me along with their loved, helped guide me in these things.

But at this time, when I walked the sidewalks outside the hospice, I often prayed that I, too, would die. I didn't think I could survive the pain. There were many friends and relatives I wanted to call, to ask them to come and sit with me, but they were working, or didn't want to see my aunt in her current condition or did not live close enough to come. Some were not close to me, and I felt that I couldn't ask that favor of them. But no matter who came and sat with me or what happened, there was nothing anyone could do. That was the worst part of it all.

Aunt Millie, who rescued me as a child when my mother could not care for me, who helped me raise my girls, the light of my life, was dying. Her strength would not let her heart stop beating though.

Everything echoed in my mind. Childhood songs, laughter, cake batter, traditions, good time, all played in my head and heart like a movie reel. She was everything good and right with the world.

But like the nursery rhyme from my youth, "All the king's horses and all the king's men couldn't put Millie together again."

It felt like the end of my childhood, my children's happy childhood, and my world.

Yet, we had a wedding coming up.

And I knew my aunt. Had she known she would have come to us and apologized. We could not be sad, not for Shannon's wedding. She would never want us to be sad or to be a burden to us.

But perhaps she did know and made a deal with God. The two of them conspired to allow us to be happy for Shannon and Mark rather than being sad for her.

The night came, and she passed away.

Now, we had both a wedding and a funeral to plan. I remember one day, either right before or right after she passed when I went to St. Helen's, the church I had grown up and been married in and met with a deacon to plan my aunt's funeral mass.

As we were talking, my daughter, Shannon called. "Hurry up, mom," she said. "You need to meet me for my final gown fitting."

It was one of the saddest times of my life, and I remember being angry at God for not allowing me to celebrate my daughter because I was grieving for my aunt. I felt sad and angry that my daughter would have to go through this hell at what should have been the happiest time of her life.

But my father said it best, as always: "What are we going to do?" He wasn't asking me; he was telling me. "We are going to have the wedding, as Aunt Millie would have wanted. That is what we are going to do. It's too bad these things are so close, but that's what we are going to do."

Ten days after the funeral, on August 5, 2015, we walked into my daughter's wedding. We had chosen a song by Rod Stewart to be played as we were announced as the parents of the bride. It was the song we would waltz into the Rochester Riverside Convention Center to, in front of 250 of our family and friends. We made the selection months before; with no idea my aunt would pass so shortly before the wedding.

But as they announced, "Mr. and Mrs. Rick Cook, parents of the bride!" the song began, and the words haunted me.

"There's a soul in the city, there's a soul in the city, watching over us tonight."

And indeed, she was watching over us that night. My Aunt Millie was there for all of us, one last time.

Rest in peace, Aunt Millie. You saved me. None of us can ever forget your goodness. You are one in a million.

Chapter Thirty:
Remembering Uncle Tom

Before we go on, I must tell you about my precious Uncle Tom, my Aunt Millie's husband, a key example of what I am trying to express in the story of the relationship between my father and me.

Through the process of telling my story I have grown and changed and feel as though I am emerging through a kind of spiritual fog or mist.

Still my tears flow; I will forever miss my wonderful family, but the beauty is that each day, despite their absence, there is still their presence. They are still "giving to me," even in death.

One true and very clear revelation is, despite my deep grief there are innumerable lessons about love and its eternal presence, and how love keeps giving to us to be found in their lives and their example to me.

While my story has focused largely on the very special and hard-to-describe ethereal bond I shared with my amazing dad, and also all the other people I've tried to "share" through my story, one mystery of love and relationship is that, as hard as we try to explain, categorize, measure or define love, it seems to slip through our grasp like trying to squeeze grains of sand in the palm of our hands. The harder we try, the more it slips through our fingers, almost refusing our inadequate attempts at definition.

Yet my life, my story would not nearly be complete if not for my attempt, however imperfect or inadequate to talk about the "other" father-like figure, who shaped and loved me and my family with so much kindness, generosity, and character that I can barely write about it. At present, my tears are flowing like a faucet. How blessed was I to be surrounded by all this goodness and love?

I must take breaks as I write these words for that is how deep my love for this man is. Being surrounded by such pure love is such a beautiful and rare thing, and my heart is overwhelmed. The sadness comes in, because as the recipient of all this goodness, it is difficult for me to talk about for three reasons: One is the feeling that, why me? Why was I chosen to receive all this love, and the second is feeling dwarfed by its presence in my life, the feeling that I can never aspire to be as good as the people that God gave to me, and lastly, now their absence in my life, now, since they have gone home to be with God, and are "missing from me" on earth.

As I try to navigate these questions and realities, it is essential to talk about what a beautiful, inspirational, kind, generous, funny, loving man my uncle was.

Whereas my father was all passion and spit-fire personality, my Uncle Tom was the "yin to his yang." He was the quiet, solid man. Methodical, he paid attention to detail, a deep thinker, who had a silly sense of humor and a heart bigger than the ocean.

He too, truly was the rock of our family. He and my aunt never had children but truly loved and supported all their nieces and nephews, especially myself, my husband and children, and my cousin, Tony and his wife, Jane, as well as all his other nieces and nephews.

My aunt and uncle's home was our refuge from any storm; our "go-to place"; the place for hundreds of family dinners and holidays. My uncle would bring the turkey downstairs in the basement to his "cutting table" where he would carve it to perfection, like an expert chef, into his 90s. No one carved turkeys and roasts like Tom did. He was the official "Mr. Fix-it"— whether it was fixing a broken toy for any of us, untangling our jewelry, sharpening all our knives; whether it was building snowmen with my kids with the joy of a ten year old, watching old movies and cartoons, or building a doll house out of an old cardboard box; giving us all buckets of coins to roll up and "help him out" then presenting us with the cash we rolled up "for him"; mock cocktails with or even maybe with a "few drops" of alcohol when we were kids. All these were a thing at Uncle Tom's house. From board games, cards, ice cream sundaes and sleepovers with friends, to cousins, picnics in their "Italian garage," dart board games, bocce, Easter egg hunts on the front lawn, outings and trips, teaching me how to bet on the horses at the racetrack, weekly scratch-off cards to "try our luck" at winning our "big million," attending all my kids events, concerts, recitals, cheerleading tournaments, soccer games, basketball games and parties, walking all over hell's half acre on 80-year-old bad feet to buy my kids the exact Pokémon card they were longing for, these were all things he did for our family. He often prayed with us and for us, took countless photographs of all of us, decorated his house for our birthdays and hosted many birthday parties for us.

He often told us stories of his youth, showing us how to savor life in every way possible, we all remember fondly his love of golf, his adored chocolate that he could eat by the pound and always sharing his love of every kind of sweets and candy, his love of old cars, showing us how to "squeeze every drop out of life" as he stated it, for all the times, all the trips he took me on as a child, all the love, all the sacrifice, all the laughs, for this I honor and remember you, Uncle Tom, as does all your family.

There can never ever be enough thanks or love to describe you, your life, or the everlasting example and impact you had upon me. I am forever grateful for you, your generosity that knew no bounds, and I am only sorry that this short explanation of the man you were can never quite cover it all...my "other father."

I love you to the moon and back.

"Who knows for whom the bells toll?" was one of your quirky and silly random sayings. Well, they toll for you, my sweet uncle, always and forever for you, my dad's very best friend on earth. Until we meet again. Forever thankful, forever grateful for you and your life.

Part Four

You are more than your thoughts, your body, or your feelings.

You are a swirling vortex of limitless potential who is here to shake things up and create something new that the universe has never seen.

— Dr. Richard Bartlett

Chapter Thirty-One: Finding Karen

My Aunt Millie was indeed one in a million as was her husband, my Uncle Tom. And my family was both loving and amazing, and I don't want to give you the impression that they were not enough. But I always dreamed of having siblings, and being adopted, I thought it might be possible.

In the winter of 2016, my Uncle Tom was still living, but not in great health, in assisted living, and Rick and I were still caring for him and my dad.

A friend on Facebook named Karen Dinolfo Ercoli, a girl I had gone to high school with, posted that she had recently reunited with a bunch of siblings she never knew she had. She, too, was adopted, and I was intrigued.

I commented on her post that I was also adopted and that years before, at the age of twenty-one, I had contacted New York State Adoptive Services to get what they called non-identifying information. They sent me the information they had, including my parents' ages, ethnic backgrounds, some of their family information such as siblings, and what they had shared of their hobbies and interests.

Much of the information they supplied was like what my adoptive parents had already shared with me. I was satisfied with what I had learned. Years later, they sent me a letter stating that New York laws had changed, and they could now share with me that I had an older sibling.

My husband had pretty much discouraged me from following up and looking into it any further. "Great, an older sibling. Diane, you don't know if they are alive or dead, male, female, where they live, or anything else. We have two kids in private schools, a mortgage, bills. What do you think you are going to do? Hire a private investigator? Then what?"

Uncharacteristically, I didn't argue.

"He's right," I thought. "Just put this out of your mind."

The chances of finding my sibling would be slim to none and hiring someone to perform a search might be too costly. As time passed, my memory of the contents of the letter faded, and the idea of a sibling seemed less and less real.

Anyway, I wrote a letter to the New York State Adoptive Services.

My friend, Karen DiNolfo Ercoli, had also recently reunited with siblings of her own. When I saw her talking about them on Facebook, I reached out to her. She told me about a friend of hers named David Guentner, who was a local genealogist. He ran a business called "Somewhere in Time Genealogy" and Karen urged me to contact him.

Later I went to breakfast with an old friend from grammar school and high school, Kathy O'Neill. "A friend I work with, a woman, also is adopted, and she contacted the New York State Adoption Registry. She is also looking for her family," she told me. She shared with me later that in the back of her mind, she thought, *What if this woman I know and Diane are sisters?* But she said nothing to me at the time. She thought the idea was much too far-fetched, a long shot at best.

But she kept staring at me. She thought she saw resemblances between me and the woman she was thinking of. Her name was Karen Zempel.

"Pancakes, omelets, toast, and bacon," said our waitress, ending our conversation.

But one new sister coming up, my friend Kathy thought.

Without knowing her thoughts, I sent the letter and I contacted David. He responded.

He was generous with his time, and his expertise proved invaluable. He told me to write another letter to the New York State Adoption Registry since it had been years since I last heard from them. In the interim, laws had changed regarding the release of information for the benefit of adoptees.

So, I did. On February 12th, a call came.

I had just left a grocery store near my home where I had been buying Valentine's balloons, cards, and candy for my two daughters. As I got into my car. I looked around at the snow falling around me like a snow globe. The flakes were fluffy and large, absorbing the sounds of the day. I looked it could turn into one of our typical upstate New York snowstorms.

My cell phone chimed. "Kathy O'Neil," it said.

Why would she be calling me now? I thought. We had recently had breakfast, but before that, we hadn't seen each other since high school.

"Hello?" I answered.

"Di, I have something to tell you. It's exciting news!"

"What Kathy?" I replied.

"I think I know who your sister is!"

"What?"

"Yes, I really think I do."

"Tell me right now," I said.

"Do you remember Karen Zempel, from Bryant and Stratton?"

"Of course, I do," I said. "She was my favorite teacher."

Suddenly, my body felt frozen, my mind racing. *Could Karen be my sister?* I thought.

I remembered her, and how I admired her right off the bat. One or two times I really stared at her. Something about her eyes, her dark Italian looks, and her petite frame made me wonder if she could somehow be related to me.

You're crazy, I'd thought at the time. *She's older, you're adopted, and an only child. What kind of goofy thoughts are these? Impossible. What made you think that?*

That moment had been thirty years before.

"Karen showed me a letter today from the Adoption Registry," Kathy said, interrupting my thoughts. "Your name was on it. You were listed as her sister."

I hesitated for about two seconds and then screamed. I had chills all over.

"Give me her phone number right now!"

Kathy gave it to me. I told her to stay on the phone with me because somehow, I knew when I got home my letter from Adoptive Services would be in my mailbox.

She stuck with me, and sure enough, the letter was among others in my mailbox. I ripped it open to find the confirmation.

"We are happy to inform you that we can disclose the name and address of your sibling. Karen Cometa Zempel."

Her address was below her name, but there was no phone number. Thanks to my friend, I already had that.

I pulled into the garage, whipped open the trunk, and nearly lost the balloons there into the night. I shut the garage door and put them back in the trunk for the moment.

I fumbled with my keys but managed to get inside. My feet, slippery from snow, nearly went out from under me as I got to the phone.

"Call Rick."

"Call Dad."

"Call Shannon."

"Call Jaimee."

These were the thoughts racing through my head and I couldn't even think straight.

Oh my God, I have a sister. I have a sister! The thought filled my mind. In my excitement, and without anything to write down the number Kathy had given me, I kept repeating it to myself over and over.

Chapter Thirty-Two: Niagara Falls

After Karen and I connected by phone on that wintery February evening a few short days before Valentine's Day, we both realized we had made plans to go to Niagara Falls that coming weekend. In our excitement, we never thought to meet up at the falls, but instead agreed to get in touch and meet up the following week.

On Sunday, ready to drive home, Rick and I decided to go to a local shopping outlet before we left. We walked around for about an hour and having exhausted all the places I wanted to see; I was ready to leave. My husband suggested we walk in a different direction.

Instead, I told him no, that if we were going to walk, I wanted to go in the opposite direction. He insisted on his plan, and I insisted on mine back, stating I did not want to go that way.

He gave in.

Not fifty yards ahead of me, sitting on a bench, was my sister, Karen! I poked Rick.

"There's my SISTER!"

"Where?" he demanded.

"Over there," I pointed to where she was sitting.

"How do you know it's her?" he asked.

"Rick! I know it is her, she was my teacher in college, and don't you think I know and remember what she looks like?"

"Yes," he replied, "But that was a long time ago. Are you SURE it's her?"

"Of course, I am," I replied.

With that, I ran over, said hello, and she jumped up off the bench and I think we were both screaming. She also knew instantly it was me! Her best friend, Gail, who was sitting there with her, had heard the story, and started to cry. Karen and I did not cry. We were both just overwhelmed and deliriously happy!

We told each other we had bought the other a gift that day, that we planned to exchange when we got back to Rochester that following week. We both thought alike on so many things.

We met the following week, and each had bought each other a bracelet. This "tandem" thinking continues to this day. Not only do we like most of the same things, but we think a lot alike, and we have uncovered similarities too significant to just be a coincidence.

Karen and I are both left-handed. Our husbands both bought our diamond engagement rings in the same shape, a pear shape, that we both love, from the same jeweler. We both were good in languages in school, despised math, are completely hopeless when it comes to having a sense of direction, and we both have zero mechanical abilities. Additionally, we both own two jewelry armoires in our bedrooms.

Upon seeing them when she came to my house for the first time, my sister exclaimed, "Diane, no one else has two jewelry armoires in their bedroom." But Karen and I do!

We both love shopping, buying clothes, and purses. We both always hated sports. We put ICE in our wine, which we know is a big "no-no," and our favorite ice cream flavor is mint chocolate chip. Both of our dear aunts left us a little bit of money, and we discovered we both took the money and bought ourselves time-shares in Orlando, Florida, which are located about three miles away from each other.

Me and my sister Karen, baking traditional Italian Christmas cookies.

We discovered one of my cousins, Annie Cassara, had been Karen's late husband Paul's boss for over 40 years at Xerox, before Paul got sick.

The list goes on and on, and the more we get to know each other, the more similarities we find.

My sister and I believe in our hearts that finding each other at a low point in both of our lives, and at the stage of our lives we were in at the time is nothing short of Divine Intervention and has been a huge blessing to each of us!

After losing my mom several years earlier and then that winter losing my close and dear Aunt Millie, I was feeling alone, and a bit lost since my older daughter had gotten married and our younger daughter was away in college.

My sister, Karen, had been caring for her husband, Paul, who had been diagnosed with early-onset Alzheimer's disease at age 54. She cared for him almost singlehandedly for ten years before his death, all while keeping her career as an English professor going strong.

I am still in awe of her strength and character in caring for her sick husband, who, for the last six years of his life, was unable to comprehend or utter a single word of speech. Right after Paul passed away, feeling lost and depressed, Karen, who had also known she was adopted, decided to investigate if she had any relatives who were also searching for her.

One month before meeting me, Karen visited a psychic. The psychic asked Karen if she knew a "Diane."

My sister responded, "No, I do not know any 'Dianes'!"

The psychic told her, "Well, you are going to meet a 'Diane,' and she is going to be very significant in your life."

We were reunited one month later.

Serendipity, there you are, again.

Karen and me, at a 1920s Flapper dance. In the few short years we've known each other, we've done so much together—trips, parties, holidays with our families, going to the casino, plays, theatre—you name it, we've done it! We've had such a blast going out, getting to know one another and each other's families.

Chapter Thirty-Three: National Television

I grew up with a local newscaster named Ginny Ryan. She got wind of my story and aired it on one of our local channels.

The night of the taping for the local channel, Karen and I were in my kitchen and Ginny had not arrived yet. Another reporter she'd sent ahead thought it might be a "good idea" if Karen and I started to do some "cooking."

Is he crazy? I thought to myself. First, I had spent all day, making sure my house looked perfect. Second, I am normally terrified of public speaking, let alone "performing" in front of a camera. Did he think Karen and I were some kind of sisterly Rachel Ray show? So, I found a sibling, and now they expected us to be "actresses" for the news as well?

My dad, who was living at the time, came to my house for his first meeting with my new sister in person. He walked into my house, knowing that reporters would be there, and they caught on film me introducing my dad to Karen, my newfound sister.

After that moment, Karen and I were giggling with each other and nervous, me more so than her, as she had been a teacher for years and taught public speaking courses. She was definitely more at ease and more used to "ad-libbing" than I was or ever will be. It was a rather nerve-wracking experience.

After I told the reporter under no circumstances would we be doing an impromptu "cooking," he guided us into my sunroom, asked us to get out some photo albums and "reminisce." Karen and I looked at each other, and it was like we had the same thought process.

Reminisce? About what? we thought. *We have known each other for two weeks!* Still in the interest of making an interesting story, and having a backdrop, which we were assured would be edited and that we would be made to look good, we tried our best to "chit-chat" while thumbing through some of my old photo albums and some of Karen's old photos, too.

I felt awkward, like it was scripted, which it was. It felt stilted, but Karen and I did the best we could.

We laughed and laughed about this later and over the past couple of years we've continued to laugh about this experience, and about how we were expected to be "actresses."

The reporter later took us back into my kitchen and told me to get out cookbooks and recipes and to talk about our common Italian heritage and maybe even about the way we both cooked our Italian "sauce."

My sister, without missing a beat, while pretending to be intently looking through a recipe box of mine, looked deep into my eyes in a serious voice says to me while the camera is rolling:

"So, Diane, how do you make your sauce? Now, do you put a little sugar in it? I hear some people put a little sugar in their sauce, and I sometimes do."

I stumbled to reply, and I think I said something to the effect of, "Yes, yes, I sometimes do as well, and I think some people even put a whole carrot in their sauce." I felt like it was the worst acting ever.

Sauce? I think this whole escapade could have been called: "Awkward Sauce."

Fast forward. We got through our local Channel 13 interview. It aired locally and turned out to be pretty cute and touching.

Karen and I thought to ourselves, *Well, wasn't that cute, and nice and heartwarming.* What we didn't bargain for was that our story would continue on, and on and on. Ginny told me, "Diane, my producers love this story, and they think it will go national!"

After that, we appeared in our local Democrat and Chronicle newspaper and the Brother Wease radio show. What a hoot that was. We sat in the radio station, early one morning up on the 8th floor of a downtown building, both decked out in cute outfits and donning our headsets. It was fun talking on live radio while Brother Wease interviewed us. We had a blast, although Wease kept such tight control over the conversation that we could barely express our thoughts and our overwhelming excitement at not only being on the radio but the fact that we had found one another. He called us "two Italian broads," much to my refined sister's chagrin. The interview ended, and once off-air, Wease was sweet and offered us a gift certificate and told us to go have breakfast at a local well-known breakfast and bakery spot.

We left the radio station giddy. I think we were laughing and literally skipping down the sidewalk; it was about 8:15 on a weekday morning. My husband, Rick, had very generously taken us down to the radio station and said he would bring us to breakfast afterward.

So, as we, the two sisters, were literally skipping down some downtown streets to our car after the interview on our way to breakfast, we looked at one another, laughed, and said: "Ok, well there was our 15 minutes of fame, wasn't that a riot?"

Little did we know, as Ginny Ryan had predicted, it was only beginning.

Because of the unusual aspects involved two sisters that were student and professor without each knowing who the other was, our story went viral.

We had reporters from several newspapers phoning us about interviews, the New York Post, the New York Times, and they published versions of our story online. We had a photographer from one of the papers, Sam Maller, come to Rochester where I was celebrating my younger daughter, Jaimee's 20th birthday at a local Kobe Japanese restaurant. Then he followed us to where I and my family were attending a play and did a photo shoot of me and Karen in the lobby where the play was showing. They actually delayed the start of the play while he was photographing us!

Me and my newly discovered sister, Karen. Here, we are holding our baby pictures for a German magazine article in 2016 where we told our story about finding each other. It was so much fun!

We had magazine writers from all over the world contact us who wanted to write our story. Most notably, a magazine from England ran our story with several pictures, and even paid each of us a small amount.

One day, while we were out shopping at our local Eastview Mall in Rochester, New York, we exited one of our favorite stores, White House Black Market, and we proceeded to sit on the couches in a waiting area of the mall. A producer from *The Ellen Show* contacted Karen and me. We talked to her through Skype and she interviewed us about our story. Although they never did get back to us, they told us that they may have wanted us to appear on Ellen's show!

The two most exciting things we did were our interview with *Good Morning America* and having our story aired on *World News* with David Muir!

In Karen's living room in Fairport, New York, I sat very close to my new sister, and we clutched each other's hands. We were primped and made up. Hair, nails, makeup, eyelashes, we were good to go for national television ready to be interviewed by reporters from *Good Morning America*. In front of us were two floodlights and a male photographer and a female interviewer. The lights burned bright, I was sweating, and very nervous. The whole experience was surreal. Time stopped.

The reporters told us once the cameras were rolling, we could not flinch, make a mistake or otherwise not be "on."

Having dealt with anxiety for most of my life, I was nervous. Not only did we have little to no preparation for what we would be asked, but the interview carried on for about 45 minutes and seemed interminable to me. Karen, knowing I have this anxiety, clutched my hand even tighter.

At one point, I could feel my mouth go dry, and my thoughts started spinning in my head, the lights were so hot, and my heart started to race a bit. I grabbed Karen's hand and squeezed even tighter and prayed I wouldn't faint or otherwise have some kind of panic attack. It felt like a long time to sit, smile, nod, answer questions, and appear relaxed and natural. Was it fun and exciting? Sure. But it was equal parts nerve-wracking and unnatural as well.

Once it aired nationally, a day or so later, my dad got a call from his nephew, Vince, who lives in Florida.

"Uncle Joey? It's Vince. I just saw you and your daughter on television!" Now whether this was that local clip of Karen and I, or one of the other television appearances we had done, I don't quite remember now, but suffice it to say, our story went everywhere over the months following our reunion.

I have a high school friend, a podiatrist, that lives in Illinois, Dr. Joe Borreggine. He texted me to say: "Diane, I was working out at my gym in Chicago, and there you were on the television!"

Despite our fame, David continued his search even after my sister and I were reunited. He pinned down our biological mother's identity. He found her name and even sent me a high school photo of her.

Can you imagine living your whole life thinking you would never see the face of your own mother? If you are adopted, you might.

This was not to take away from my adoptive family. I had a great mother and father who raised me, adored me, and who I adored as well.

However, there is always the curiosity about your biological family or parents. My birth mother had passed away a few years before and discovering that made me sad. My intention in my search had not been to meet her, but to, at least, learn about family health and our background. But her death ensured that I would never have that chance.

The contact with my sister was a bonus for sure. I'd always wanted a sibling, and sharing our lives, even at this late date, was a blessing.

But David did not give up. His search was extremely accurate. He spent a lot of time researching my background to find out the truth behind my birth and the circumstances surrounding it.

The more David learned, the more open my family was. My adoptive dad "suddenly" found my legal adoptive paperwork, and my biological mother's name was right there.

In 2018, David produced yet another miracle for me. I initially wasn't all that interested in who my birth father was. I had a great relationship with my adoptive father, and he would never not be "dad" to me. I decided to attempt to find my biological father's identity.

Through extensive searches, David found his name, and that he was also deceased. Through the process, I located five more half-siblings, three sisters and two brothers. I was over the moon with excitement! I have David to thank for all of this.

Chapter Thirty-Four: Christmas 2018, The Jim Brickman Concert and "The Gift"

In December of 2018, I was at a Jim Brickman concert at our local auditorium theatre with my husband, Rick. Little did I know, on that beautiful and evening just about two weeks before Christmas, like his song, "The Gift," there was another unimaginable "gift" I was about to receive. Sarah Brightman also sang that evening.

Rick and I went to the concert dressed to the nines and felt very festive. It was a fun evening, and a great concert.

When I got home it was about 11 p.m. and I noticed several messages on my phone. I glanced at them and saw that my genealogist friend, David Guentner, who had helped me reunite with my sister Karen, had messaged me.

He stated he was certain he had found not only my biological father and his identity, but that he had contact information for some of his relatives. I was excited and confused, but never could have anticipated what would happen next.

David's messages contained two or three names and numbers. I was confused as to who these people were. Since it was so late, but I had ultimate faith in David, and I thought to myself, *What the heck, I am just going to call to see if I can reach anyone!*

I told Rick my plan, but he instantly told me not to do it.

"Can't you wait until the morning?" he said. "It's late."

"Rick, are you kidding me right now? I have my biological dad's relatives' contact numbers! No, I am not waiting!"

I excitedly punched in the number for a "Linda." I think David told me that she was my dad's wife. I was so nervous as I dialed. What would this person think of me, calling at this hour? Would she believe my story? Would she hang up on me? Would she even listen? Would she think I was some crazy person?

I dialed anyway.

"Hello?"

"Hello, Linda?"

"Yes?"

"Linda, my name is Diane DiProspero Cook. I hope you are sitting down. I am sorry to be calling you this late, but I could not wait. I have a story to tell you, but please do not think I am crazy, and please do not hang up on me."

I proceeded to tell Linda all about David Guentner, finding my sister, Karen, and how David believed I was the daughter of her husband, Ken. I told her where I lived and grew up, where I went to school, who my family was, and many other things. I think I blurted out my story in about 3 minutes flat.

I was so thankful she listened to me and did not hang up on me.

"Oh my God," said Linda. I knew right then she believed me and my heart was racing and hands were shaking. There was about a 10-second pause, and then she said calmly, "Well, Ken always said he had a 'kid' out there somewhere."

"Oh my God," I said in reply.

Then Linda spoke for a while and told me many things about my biological father and proceeded to tell me she was his second wife. He apparently had had 4 children, 3 of whom were related to me, and she and Ken had 2 more children. So, on that magical night before Christmas, I learned I had three more half-sisters, another named Karen, the oldest, Janet, and Kevin, from my biological Dad's first wife and Ken and Beverly from his second wife, Linda.

"WHAT?" was all I could say.

I was in complete shock. As Linda tried to fill me in on the family tree and all the siblings I had, my mind was spinning! Just a few short years before, and for my entire life I had been an "only child" wishing for siblings! I had found Karen just two years before, and now this?

My younger daughter and her boyfriend, Justin, were downstairs, and I shouted out to them as loud as I could:

"Jaimee, your mother has five MORE SIBLINGS! OH.MY.GOD."

I felt like I had won the lottery.

My close immediate family was deceased; I was so heartbroken still. But, now THIS? I couldn't believe this was happening. I was so overjoyed, but of course, cautious. Who knew what these siblings would think of me, or if they would even want to accept me or get to know me? I couldn't worry about those things at that moment, though. All I knew was, another miracle was happening to me!

Suddenly Linda interrupted me. I am not sure, while on the call with me, how she had managed to contact her daughter, Beverly, and one of the other half sisters, Janet, but she did.

"Diane, Diane, I am getting messages from my daughter and her half-sister and they want to talk to you, they keep beeping in on the phone line; they are messaging me frantically—can we hang up so that they can phone you?"

"Of course," was my immediate answer. It had to be close to midnight by this time.

Truth be told, I had messaged another contact given to me by David about a day before. It was, unbeknownst to me, my new younger brother, Ken. Ken had contacted his sisters, and they were now trying to get ahold of their mom and find out what was going on.

As soon as I hung up the phone, my phone rang. "Hello?"

"Hello, this is Diane," I said, my heart racing.

"Diane, this is your SISTER, Beverly."

"Oh my God!" And also on the line came another voice: "And your sister, Janet!"

We talked for at least an hour, maybe two.

All I knew was that I was on cloud nine.

My sisters? What? Thank you, God. I thought to myself.

Aunt Millie told me just before she died: "Honey, something will come up. I just know it. Something will come up." Did she and the others know I had some siblings out in the world?

That I will never know.

Well, something sure did come up, Aunt Millie. You all had to leave me. I feared and dreaded it. You all had to go. Your time with me, Rick and our girls was up. There was no stopping it.

But look at what God gave me. All my siblings and I found each other. I was not alone.

Chapter Thirty-Five: Honor Flight

The man who would be forever my dad no matter what I found about my biological family was one of the World War II vets offered the opportunity to go on an Honor Flight trip to Washington, D.C. The first time it was mentioned, we were out to dinner at Jeremiah's, a restaurant in Penfield, with my sister, Karen, and some of her friends from work.

At first, he declined. "Why do I gotta go look at graves of dead guys?" he asked me. "And I'm not up for that trip."

"Okay, Dad," I said.

I didn't really think about it until around a year later, after a long, cold, and boring winter that left him homebound, he surprised us by saying he wanted to go.

"That's great, Dad," I told him. We were happy and excited. My husband, Rick, would accompany him to make sure the trip went smoothly.

Me and my daughter, Shannon, with my dad. How we all adored him, and he adored us! This picture was taken at his last (unbeknownst to us) birthday party at my house. He was 92 years old here...never looked his age!

A couple of days before they were supposed to leave, he started to hedge about going. Early mornings were tough for him anyway, and it would be a rigorous trip for anyone.

Especially my dad. He had a history of heart problems, took diuretics and blood thinners daily, and suffered from COPD and other issues.

"You can cancel, Dad," I told him. "If you're not sure about it, maybe you should."

But my dad was a man of his word. If he said he would do something or made plans of any type, he would not cancel unless he absolutely had to.

"I don't want to disappoint Rick," he told me. Of course, Rick was going for him, not the other way around.

It didn't matter to dad. The ball was rolling, and they were set to go.

When I went over to his house the night before they were to leave, there were Honor Flight things everywhere: shirts, buttons, and their itineraries. They were both excited to go. Rick slept at his house that night so he would be able to get him up and to the airport before 5 a.m.

They left.

I don't really remember communicating with Dad or Rick too much once they got to Washington as it was a quick one-day trip. It was jammed packed from the moment they landed until they went to bed late that night. I am sure I must have texted Rick and talked to Dad, briefly, and I heard it was quite a reception for the men.

Rick told me that they bent over backward showering our WWII heroes with food, ceremonies, speeches, and honored them every possible way that they could. My dad was tired, but he echoed these sentiments, and we, of course, got the full rundown about how wonderful the trip had been when he got back to Rochester on Sunday afternoon.

When he returned, the entire extended family waited for him at the Rochester Regional Airport. Once he got off the plane and we all greeted him, I noticed something: he had a deep purple bruise on his right ear, the color of eggplant.

"Rick, what happened to Dad's ear?"

"It's no big deal. He had a little fall in the hotel room before we left, about 5 this morning."

"You're sure he's okay?"

"A nurse from Honor Flight checked him out and said everything is fine."

I knew better and blowing it off as no big deal made me angry. For a man my dad's age, with his health history, any fall could turn into a problem. No one else seemed worried, but I was.

He often had bruises covering his arms because of being on Coumadin, and even slight bumps caused bruising and bleeding, let alone a fall like the one Rick had described.

But we got him home a couple of hours later. He was exhausted, but more worried about a small cut on his arm from the fall and wanted to get that checked out. So, we fed him lunch, and then Rick took him to the Urgent Care.

I went home to catch up on my chores, thinking I would see about a late dinner for the three of us if my dad was up to it.

The staff at the Urgent Care re-bandaged his arm but he declined dinner.

"I'm exhausted," he said.

"You're sure you are okay?" I asked. I didn't want to leave him home alone.

"I'm fine. Just really tired," he told me.

The next day, a Monday, I went to work and so did Rick. I called my dad to check on him.

"How are you feeling?" I asked him.

"I'm still tired, and I don't feel great," he answered.

"Do you want to go to the doctor?"

"No."

I called that evening again, and we repeated our conversation. He did not feel great but did not want to go to the doctor then either.

The next day repeated the same scenario. He even sounded out of breath but did not want to go to the doctor or the hospital, despite admitting he still did not feel well.

I headed home after work and then to the gym. While I was still in the parking lot, my phone rang.

"I'm not feeling well at all," my dad said.

"Okay," I said. "I'm calling the ambulance."

I sped to his house after letting Rick and my daughter know what was going on.

When I arrived, he was already on a stretcher in the breezeway, the paramedics checking his vitals. They loaded him in the ambulance, and normally I would've ridden with him. Instead, I stayed back, staring at the back windows of the emergency vehicle.

Time stood still. I just peered into the windows as they questioned him and checked him. I could see them talking, but I could not hear what they said. Everything slowed down. A paramedic interrupted my staring, opened the door, and came and asked me a few questions.

They were trying to determine if he'd had a stroke.

Within minutes, we were following the ambulance to Strong Memorial Hospital. It was the go-to place for neurology and the closest one to his house.

We waited in the emergency room for what seemed like hours.

I kept walking over to the security guard at his podium and asking, "Any word on Joseph DiProspero?"

"No, ma'am, we will let you know as soon as we hear something," he said over and over.

We were all on pins and needles.

Finally, a physician came out to talk to us. Her words held a certain urgency, and went on to explain that she had, "good news and bad news."

"Your father has what we call a subdural hematoma, or in layman's terms a bleed that occurs on the top of your brain."

I wanted to cry. The blood rushed from my head to my feed, and everything seemed to go blank. It felt like my head was empty and my body disappeared. I was numb.

My whole family stood behind me, and responded with a chorus of questions:

"What does that mean?"

"What's happening?"

"What? What?"

I shushed them and concentrated on what the doctor was saying. I wanted to know what was next.

"We'll need to do surgery to remove the pressure from your father's brain," she said. "We have to stop the bleeding and remove any blood that has collected there."

It came down to me. I had to decide whether to put my father, a 92-year-old with some serious health issues, through this surgery. The surgeon seemed confident, but I had only minutes to decide.

"Yes," I said. "Let's do it."

As I filled out consent forms, I felt like it was all taking too long. I wanted to shout, "Go! Go! Hurry up!"

Of course, she reassured me they were prepping my dad for surgery. What I did not know was that he'd lost consciousness in the triage room, and they were racing to stabilize him and get him into surgery as fast as they could.

"You will have your dad back," the doctors assured me, then disappeared.

We could do nothing but wait. Dad went into surgery at 9 p.m. and came out at 1 a.m. We saw him shortly after, probably around 2 a.m.

I'll never forget the way he looked. There were tubes, drainage tubes I would later learn, coming out of him. Wires ran to equipment I had never seen. His head was shaved and bandaged. A breathing tube, deep in his throat, fed him oxygen from a hissing, clicking machine.

I felt sick.

Even his open-heart surgery, some 32 years earlier, had been nothing compared to this.

Progress was slow. He had good days when some of the tubes and wires were removed, and there were fewer things attached to him. Still, ten days after surgery, dad had not regained consciousness. There was talk of unplugging the machines that were left.

I didn't want to think about that.

No, he didn't go through all this for nothing, I thought.

I did not want the Honor Flight to have been dad's "last flight." My dad was my entire world. It was him and I against the world. He knew it, I knew it, and we lived it. We were best buddies.

My mom was his wife, I was his best friend, and his baby girl. The fight we fought, the one to try to help my mom, to free her from prescription drug addiction and depression, to make her happy, was a fight I'm not sure we ever won.

Even when she sort of stopped taking pills, her body had deteriorated and was ravaged with sickness.

The irony of the Honor Flight was not lost on me. He married my mom on an Army base in Walla Walla, Washington, during World War II. This trip to honor World War II and other Veterans could not be his last.

"You watch, Diane. Your dad is such a wonderfully religious man, he will wake up on Easter Sunday," someone told me.

The holiday was fast approaching, but even though we tried to cling to it tightly, we as a family started to lose hope.

Then it happened: on Easter Sunday, I sat with him, massaging his hands, and like an actress in a movie, I said to him:

"Dad, I know you're in there. If you can hear me, please squeeze my hand or wiggle a finger or toe."

This wasn't the first time I'd asked, but I kept trying. This time, he wiggled his toes. I thought I was seeing things, but it was real.

He could hear me!

Hallelujah! I called my husband and the nurse. I cried. Of course, like a baby taking their first step, at first dad would not "perform" and wiggle his toes again.

The nurse and even my husband gave me a look, the look of doubt. They thought I'd hallucinated.

But then he did it again. Within a few hours, he was squeezing my hand. I called my daughters and told them.

It was an on and off again thing, but we had hope.

Chapter Thirty-Six: Dad's Calling

The days and weeks that followed Dad's surgery were the most painful and grueling nightmare for him and all of us. We spent days sitting by his side, listening to doctors give us varying reports on his progress that changed sometimes by the hour, good, then bad, then good again. Any little positive sign gave us so much hope but was often dashed by some unforeseen setback.

When a person suffers a brain bleed, there can still be some residual blood left behind, even after the surgery to remove the blood that had collected. This "extra" blood, is foreign to the body, and the brain does not like it at all and can result in seizures while it is being reabsorbed. I arrived one day to find Dad having a grand mal seizure after they decided they would try taking him off anti-seizure medications. I guess the doctors thought he was doing so well and that he was out of the danger zone, but they were wrong. I will never forget the horrific sight.

Doctors and nurses flew into his room to assist, and I stood there horrified and frozen before someone shooed me out. This is just one example of the many horrible things that Dad had to endure during those three weeks.

It was an endless stream of doctors trying to clear his lungs that would fill up with congestion and suctioning them. He would wince with the pain while they did this. His hands, I will never forget, were in these mesh "mittens" to keep him from pulling tubes out when he wasn't quite coherent. He begged us for a drink, but because he had a feeding tube and due to the risk of pneumonia through aspiration, we could offer him little but a few scarce chips of ice, and that was only granted to him after days of suffering blistering thirst.

I would have to exit the room to sob because he was suffering in the most excruciating way, and there wasn't anything I could do to help him. I was devastated, traumatized, exhausted, heartbroken, and frustrated. I wanted to tear out my hair, scream, and cry. No help came for him or me. It was torture I wouldn't have wished on my worst enemy.

I could not and have not ever been able to forgive myself for not being able to help him in any way. I felt in some ways like I must be the cause of his suffering. Surely, I should have been able to fix this, as I told myself my dad would have fixed it for me and never allowed me to suffer in this cruel unthinkable way.

On the day Dad was doing his "best," about three weeks after his accident and surgery, we were preparing for him to have, yet, one more surgery the following Monday. For him to leave the hospital, he needed to be able to eat. The doctors determined that his swallowing function still was not where it should be, and decided he would need a feeding tube, and assured us it might be not permanent, but that he would need this to be released from the hospital to go to a rehab facility.

The doctors came into his room on a Thursday evening and explained everything. It upset him to hear he would need this surgery, and he was not happy about it at all. He understood what the surgery would involve and seemed to gloss over or maybe not fully accept he had just survived brain surgery!

I gently reminded him of that fact, and that this would be a minor procedure in comparison, that the tube would hopefully not be permanent, and that he could get out of the hospital at some point.

Both of us knew it was not going to be easy, and I think he understood that he might never be his old self again. He had been knocked down hard this time, and I think the thought of that feeding tube, and the thought of many months of grueling rehab, with no promise of getting back to normal was a huge blow. He was exhausted.

We decided together that night, with his doctors to wait it out through the weekend and see about surgery on Monday morning. I think my dad knew at that point that with or without that surgery he wasn't going to make it. He echoed that sentiment to me during the three weeks when he would be in and out of consciousness. He looked at me one day and said: "I don't think I am going to make it."

"Don't talk that way, Dad," I said. "Look at all you have been through! You will make it, you are strong, we need you, and I will take care of you."

Well, Friday came, and Dad had his "best day." We got him up and dressed and into a wheelchair. Rick took him outside on the hospital patio, and he enjoyed the fresh air. It was April. I was there all day, but just as Rick was going to take him outside, Rick told me to go home. I said goodbye. Little did I know that would be the last time I saw him awake.

I went home. I waited for Rick. Rick never came. Rick had gone out after the hospital to meet a couple of friends for a drink. We were both exhausted and burned out. I got a message from Rick's sister that his mom had fallen and broken her pelvis. I was getting frantic as I couldn't reach him. When he finally called me, I told him to head over to another local hospital where his mom was. He got home very late. I echoed my earlier feeling that I should go back to see Dad. Rick told me no, they were getting him ready for bed and I should go in the morning.

Rick finally got home from visiting his mother around 11:30 on April 28, 2017. I was exhausted and we exchanged some not-so-nice words, as I had an exam I had registered for, and Rick wanted me to go take the test in the morning. I said: "Who will be with Dad?"

He snapped at me, and said: "Someone will be there, just go take your test!"

Too exhausted to think clearly, we argued, and I told him no, I wasn't going to take my test.

Then, in a fit of frustration, Rick said, "Just go take your test! It's not like your dad is going to DIE tonight!"

I went to bed and fell into a deep sleep.

At midnight the phone on my nightstand rang. I saw the number to Strong Memorial Hospital, which I knew all too well, pop up. I knew it could not be good. In my fogginess, I practically knocked the phone off the nightstand:

I answered it.

"Mrs. Cook?"

"Yes," I said.

"There's been an incident."

"What? What's happened?"

"Your father, Joseph DiProspero."

My heart stopped cold.

The doctor explained to me that a nurse had checked my dad and found everything to be fine: his pulse, blood pressure, everything. Then twenty minutes later, someone walked by his room and found him face down and unresponsive.

Chapter Thirty-Seven: Ascension

I frantically made phone calls the night Dad passed away, to my daughter, Shannon, and my cousin, Tony, in Las Vegas. It was near midnight that night of April 28, 2017, and coincidentally it was my Grandpa Tony's (long since deceased) birthday as well as his only grandson, my cousin, Tony, who I was trying to reach to tell him the news about my dad.

Truth be told, Dad, the fighter he was, had not died but was clinging to life.

When we got to the hospital the doctors had given us a number to call and said they would meet my husband and me and bring us to where Dad was.

As they promised they came and brought us to where we needed to be but to be honest, I remember almost nothing of that walk, how many doctors there were, two, I think, what they looked like or their names. I was in shock. I remember standing in front of them and barely hearing what they were telling me. But they did ask us if we wanted CPR to continue, after explaining to us that that had given Dad twenty-six shocks to his heart, endless rounds of CPR, and then they explained to me that if they were to continue, it would do little good and he would, in essence, be brain dead. Of course, I told them no, I did not want them to continue.

We were eventually allowed into the room where Dad was lying on a table. It was a horrific sight to me. My beautiful dad was bloated. There was dried blood on the side of his face, coming out of the corner of his mouth. His stomach was hugely distended, and he had a breathing tube. They asked us to leave the room then took out the tube, and then we returned to his bedside.

All I remember is throwing my entire body over his belly and crying out loud. I did not even recognize my own voice. I could not stop crying and then was angry at myself because I wondered if Dad could still hear me, and knew what was happening and maybe I was upsetting him? I was told the dying can still hear. I tried to calm myself down because I knew it wasn't fair to him.

But I was crying too hard, and I was saying over and over: "I tried to save you, Dad, I tried, I tried to save you, I am so sorry, I couldn't do it."

This went on for quite some time and there, literally, must have been ten people, a mix of doctors and nurses in this crowded room. At that moment my sadness turned in one second, and not because I was ungrateful to these health care workers who were doing all that they could, but because they knew Dad was all but dead, and they did not give me the courtesy of my privacy. They stood there saying nothing. I screamed, "Everybody OUT!"

They fled. I still have a hard time with this. They tried to help my dad, yes, but when I got there, only a faint breath remained. They did not know to even excuse themselves or to say "sorry." I just wanted to be alone with my father.

I think Rick was right behind me, he must have been, but I remember very little. Later, I would be so angry, even as I was that night, that they gave my dad all those shocks and did things to him, knowing he couldn't survive, but this was also our fault. My dad never wanted to think about DNRs and end-of-life matters. During his ordeal in the hospital, we were asked about it once and once only, and he did have a living will and some DNR, end-of-life directives through his doctor's office years ago but had never updated it.

We were asked once during his ordeal and brain surgery, and someone was supposed to get back to us about it. They never did, and we were embroiled day to day with his care for those three weeks while he was clinging to life and having one crisis after another. The health care professionals failed us, in that they forgot to follow up about this issue with us, and we also forgot as we were just trying to manage his care, be his advocate, and be with him as much as we could.

The 26 shocks, the endless CPR, and the re-intubation must have been horrific for him, and it tortures me to think about these things, on top of all the other suffering my 92-year-old dad had to endure. His ribs were even broken.

After I managed to somewhat calm myself, my daughter, Shannon, and her husband arrived, and they wanted to go in to see my dad.

After that, we were asked to leave the room. My dad was going to be moved to another room where we could stay with him, and they would call us when they got him moved.

We were eventually taken to him, and we, basically, sat with him until he died. We sat for what felt like an eternity. We just sat crying, silent and watching. After a couple of hours, slowly we noticed Dad's lips bluing, he was getting paler. I kept touching, his arms, his hands, his face. I kissed him.

Finally, around 1 a.m. my daughter was getting nervous, as was I.

"Dad!" She said to my husband, Rick, "What is going on?"

My husband asked: "What do you mean?"

Shannon said what I was thinking. "How long are we going to just sit here? Is Papa gone? What is going on, and why isn't anyone coming in to check on us or on him?" She asked Rick to go get someone immediately.

I agreed with her. My husband hesitated, and I was getting angry again. I said the same: "Why isn't anyone coming by to see what's going on, to ask how we are?"

We, literally, could not tell if dad was still breathing or not. If he was, it was so faint that we could not even sense it.

Finally, Rick was able to grab a doctor out in the hall who then said he would have to go find someone else to determine my dad's "status."

Finally, a PA showed up. He told us he was going to assess my dad. He looked my dad over, he checked his eyes, he touched him. He checked his feet. He then rubbed Dad's chest/sternum very hard and then he called out: "JOSEPH!"

He waited. "JOSEPH!"

He called again one last time: "JOSEPH!"

Dad did not respond. We all sat crying. We looked at the clock. The doctor looked at the clock.

He said to us: Time of death: April 29th, 2:00 a.m.

My heart also stopped beating at that moment. I felt a weird sense of spirits in the room. I had the sense my dad's mother, who died when he was only 4, was there and my mother, but I said nothing to the others in the room.

Later, I saw a psychic. She told me many things she could not have known. I did not know her. I had never met her, nor did she know my name before we spoke. She immediately spoke of my father. At first, she said she was getting a message from a man who loved me very, very much. A man who had recently been on a trip (his Honor Flight trip). She saw him on long sidewalks. Rick had pushed him along long sidewalks in Washington D.C. to see all the monuments. She told me he was proud of me, and how I had fought for him, she also spoke of a medication error, which, the night dad passed, he was given a new drug to help him sleep that I had objected to, and this drug we later found out had every contraindication for a man with all the health issues he had, but I was silenced by a haughty, young physician's assistant.

They gave him the drug anyway, and he was dead four hours later.

I later found out, that while this drug probably didn't kill him that night, it may have been enough to contribute to his death. He likely died of a pulmonary embolism or heart attack as his already weakened and compromised heart, from years of heart disease most likely gave out under the strain of all he had been through.

There is one thing the psychic told me that really blew me away and sent shivers down my spine but also comforted me too. She said: "Your dad heard your prayers the night he died."

That's odd, I thought to myself, because while we sat next to his bed that night, and I sat there, sad, crying, silent at other times and, if I prayed, I did not do so out loud.

So, I happened to be telling this story about the psychic to my daughter, Shannon.

"Mom," she said. "Mark and I prayed with Papa that night."

"What do you mean?" I asked her.

"Mom, remember when you asked me and Mark, did we want a few minutes in the room alone with Papa, and we told you, 'yes'? Well, you and Dad walked out of the room for a few minutes, and Mark and I said the "Our Father" with him.

"Your dad did not want to go," the psychic told me when I asked her about the night my father died.

"Your mother and your grandmother were there. He only relented when they told him it was his time."

There were so many other signs. Even in death, he was determined to communicate with us, to let us know he heard us, and that he was ok.

She told me he said he will never leave me, and that he sits at my kitchen counter and watches over me always. That's my dad. Unfailing, loyal, and never let me down. Even death does not separate us.

I knew he didn't want to go, to leave me, Rick, and my daughters, but he followed God's will to the last, even when it was his time to go.

Despite being orphaned at a young age and the difficult circumstances of his youth and upbringing, my dad always had a spirit of giving and caring for others. I think it was in his DNA.

Sometimes is it upbringing and nurture that make us who we are. Others, it is the collective memories, experiences, and the character of others in our family that is coded and passed down to us, giving us those traits innately.

Certainly, my dad's sisters were good people who tried their best to raise him and his brothers when their parents were gone. But life was hectic, and they had their own children to raise as well. Up until he was 13, my dad's father was around, but he was stressed and working long hours, trying to support his children while recovering from the fact that he'd lost his own wife.

I was much luckier in many ways. The dedication and loyalty I witnessed going up were burned into my memory and my heart. My dad answered his call always, to be present for others and to be kind and giving.

Growing up in Catholic schools, I was taught that each of us has a calling in life, a purpose. For most of my life, I struggled as others do to find what my "call" was. "They" told us that if we really listened and opened our hearts, Jesus would tell us what that call was for each of us, and what our purpose for living was meant to be.

At first, I thought my call was to finish college and become a speech-language pathologist, but I quit for what I know now were silly reasons. I was immature and struggling with figuring out what I wanted to do for a "career." I always regretted that decision.

The summer after I quit college, I was very depressed and did not know where to turn or what I would do next. I do not know exactly why I decided to go to Bryant & Stratton, except I knew I had to do something.

I needed something to enable me to get a job. While I was excellent in shorthand, I was never a good typist, but I willed myself to master it through hours and hours of practice and positive affirmations.

So, I went to Bryant and Stratton College, where I met Karen, who I would later discover was my sister.

Sometimes God whispers in our ears, and others, he shouts. I have learned there is always divine intervention if we are receptive to being guided.

Still, I wasn't really satisfied with my "call." I spent years working in various law firms as a secretary, a stenographer at the New York Attorney General's office, and many other jobs along the way. I still wondered what God's plan for me could be.

His plan turned out to be the blessing of raising my two daughters.

My various jobs taught me things like persistence and making the best of less-than-ideal situations. I was also able to give back to my wonderful family and take care of each of them in their final years before they passed away.

But something inside me was still not fulfilled.

I feel like this book, now, is my call. I have gone through all these things so I can share them with you, along with my gratitude for the deep blessings I have experienced.

They taught me about values: Humor. Resilience, Tradition. Religion. Rituals, Honesty, Loyalty, Persistence, Tenacity. Character. Love, a healthy dose of Catholic guilt, and lots of nagging.

This is my legacy. These were the gifts I was given every day, Even the nagging was a "gift." It takes not only a "village" to raise a child, and I always had my whole extended family, but it also takes an enormous amount of persistence and energy. The energy, I later learned in raising my girls takes a type of daily "digging deep" and a conscious effort to nag kids about health habits, manners, getting them to do their schoolwork, going to church or other services, and basically to help mold them into decent, caring, loving, conscientious people is an enormous job.

They were hard workers, and God and family were everything to them. The gifts they instilled are more priceless than gold or diamonds, and the experiences I have had make me richer than a king or queen. These experiences, these are the "things," the family times, that are so sadly absent in the lives of so many children today. I call it an anemic type of upbringing and to me one of the many causes of why our world is changing for the worse.

They are not unique to that generation of survivors during the Depression and World War II and post-World War era, only they are unique in that this is *my* story and *my* family. I have always been amazed at the resilience and character of this generation, and so grateful these were my folks, my people, that God and fate had chosen, and hand-picked for me.

Despite my mother's problems, her health issues, and addiction, she triumphed finally, after my children were born. Despite frail health, and only a limited amount of life left in her ravaged body, she was determined, and succeeded, in her quest to be the most amazing grandmother to them.

We tried our best, given her frail health to enjoy whatever we could with her. There were family dinners, parties, and holidays. We managed a couple of short trips and one very memorable one in Florida, where we rented a condo and spent three glorious weeks in Marco Island. This trip always stands out in my mind as one of the best vacations I have ever had, and I will never forget my parents' joy at all of us being together and enjoying the sunshine, the pool, and even a little river cruise to see lemurs and the alligators.

In classic Joseph DiProspero-style, about forty-five minutes into our river cruise, having spotted maybe one or two lemurs, and in the 90-plus-degree heat, our guide started telling us about how the monkeys really liked chicken.

My dad whispered, "I like chicken, too. Let's get the hell off this boat."

We all laughed.

"Monkeys," he scoffed. "I want to go eat chicken. I'm hungry!"

This brought gales of laughter from all of us.

That was Dad. He was the classic Italian man. *Feed me, I'm hungry, and I don't care about these monkeys!* It was always about the food, which made us chuckle.

During the years my mother was ill and had to be on portable oxygen, my dad cared for her lovingly and doted over her. Her doctors and even my mom said, had it not been for my father she never would have survived as long as she did. She passed away in 2003 after a struggle with diabetes, macular degeneration, and heart failure at age 79.

My girls were just 10 and 7 years old at the time.

But this is not the end of this part of my story. Not yet.

Chapter Thirty-Eight: Dreamworks

July 7, 2019

I found myself dozing off on my couch, and then I started dreaming. Everything was gray, and the night surrounding me was desolate and ominous. I did not feel scared, even though I was all alone and barefoot. In the distance, I could see a large building.

The wind came up, and instantly the gust increased in strength. A tornado? A hurricane? I did not know, because I didn't know where I was. I felt lifted, nearly carried away like Dorothy in *The Wizard of Oz.* Tossed in the air, I tumbled through the sky toward a building I could see getting closer and closer.

I swung my arms and legs. Although the wind whipped around me, I couldn't tell if it was hot or cold. I fought as I flew, knowing I needed to get inside the shelter, but the wind was powerful, and had absolute control over where I was headed.

I could see my parents inside. I struggled to get to them, and finally made it. Inside, the building appeared to be a hospital, but there was an escalator, and when we reached the top, we were leaving the odd building.

I watched them walk, hand in hand, in front of me, silent. They were both in their sixties and looked very healthy. My mother had her hair done perfectly and was wearing an orange pantsuit that looked beautiful on her.

My dad bent to buckle her shoe; shoes much more modern than what she would typically wear. The heels were higher than she liked, the bottoms made of cork, the tops made of light brown leather.

My dad looked up at me and said, "What?"

He was trying to communicate with me through my dream.

"Don't you think your mom looks young, vibrant, and attractive? Don't you think she should wear these shoes?"

I didn't answer.

"I always take care of your mother. Didn't I always? I bought these beautiful shoes for her."

He seemed happy, proud to be caring for her again as he always had in real life. Still smiling, my dad seemed to want my opinion about my mother and my affirmation that he was, indeed, being a good husband.

It was his message for me, and what he wanted me to know.

They continued walking, and my mother turned toward me. We leaned toward each other, kissing one another on the cheek as if in a greeting or a goodbye. I wanted to take it all in: her beauty, the softness of her cheek, and the love between us. I don't remember kissing my dad, although I must have.

They were a few steps ahead, and I don't remember them saying goodbye, but they seemed determined to exit the building.

My mom and dad turned to smile at me, and I understood they had to go. I wondered if I would ever see them again.

Then I jolted awake. I was at home, and the clock told me it was 11:30 p.m. I was still on the couch; my husband was upstairs sleeping. My heart pounded in my chest, not from fear, but because I felt stunned. The dream left me feeling both happy and sad, and it had seemed so real, so life-like.

I realized it wasn't a dream, or even just a vision. It was a visit from my parents, letting me know they were together, well, and happy. They wanted me not to just know it, but to believe it because I saw them for myself.

Mine was not the only dream. I include here a letter I got from my daughter:

Hey Mom,

So, I know you are so sad and heartbroken about Papa. I am too. He is always on my mind, and I know he's always on yours, Jaimee's and Dad's. What I wanted to tell you though was that I had a dream the other night. It was so vivid. I am sure this was more than a dream. Papa came to me. He told me to tell you and all of us that he is okay where he is. He wants us to know that even though he is good and happy, if he were given the choice, he would have stayed with us longer. He wants us to know he had to go. His mother, Mary and your mom came that night to take him. They told him how difficult the road would have been if he stayed here, and they could not allow him to stay. He would not have had a life of quality. It would have been such an enormous struggle with so much suffering.

No one would have wanted him to endure it. Well, we know how stubborn Papa was. He wasn't willing to listen at first. It was a real struggle the night he died. Remember the doctors did CPR and administered twenty-six shocks to his weary heart. He returned to us at least two times, because he kept telling them "No!" for we all needed him! Jesus was there and extended his hand to Papa.

Papa loved us all so fiercely, so much so he hesitated even when Jesus reached out to him. And yes, he said he was scared, but mostly worried about all of us. Jesus smiled and hugged Papa and told him we would all be alright, and that he, Papa, had done enough in his early life to help not only us, but so many people. In my dream, Papa said Jesus told him he was proud of the life he lived and that he had been a good man. Papa said he was sorry for certain things, for some mistakes he thought he had made in his life, and even a few small regrets.

Next, Papa wanted to tell us all that he was told he still had to pass through certain levels before ultimately reaching heaven, but it would not be much longer and he would be there finally, in Heaven and at peace, surrounded by all his loved ones who passed before him. Papa spoke to me in that dream to assure us he is watching over all of us every day, and he will not leave us. Although his body could not hang on any longer, and although we cannot see him, he sees us every day. He said, for us, time will seem very long on earth, but in heaven there is no time. It will seem quick to Papa, the time until we will all be reunited in heaven.

My dream was clear. I heard and saw my Papa's face. He spoke to me. You know, Mom, how Papa was scared we would forget him? Well, I told him that would never happen, and in two years now since he has been gone, he cannot believe, in his view from heaven, how much he was loved! He kind of smiled when he told me that, and I saw tears in his eyes. The reason he was so surprised is not because he doubted just how much we loved him; Papa did not realize the full impact his life had on all of us, and so many other people. He said all his questions were answered when he passed from this life. All doubts, all questions and all the things we go through while we are living such as the choices we make, our deeds and experiences are explained and answered when we die.

Papa understands his life with clarity now! This he says is the glory of Heaven. We will always be loved and always be his family. He wants us as he told you, Mom, to have a good life and he will be here on the other side waiting for us. He will be waiting with open arms one day when we all come home. Until then, he is sending you and all of us his love, always.

Well, I hope this somehow soothes your heart knowing these things. I know it helped me and I wanted to share it with you.

Love, Shannon

Me and my girls, all grown up.

My younger daughter, Jaimee, posted a note on Facebook while she was away at college, honoring my dad, her grandfather, on the day he passed. I know she would want her voice heard and her love for her grandfather shared in this memoir.

April 29, 2017, Facebook

Today I'm deeply sorry to say I lost not only my Papa, but my best friend and a man who was a second father to me and my sister.

Papa, I can't believe I'm even writing this post because, just yesterday, Mom was telling me how you had the best day yet, and I couldn't wait to come home and see you next week.

Less than a week ago, we talked to you on the phone and my mom said to you, "Papa, tell Jaimee you love her. It's very important. She's at school and wants to hear your voice," and you, with your undying strength managed to say in the softest voice, "Jaimee, I love you." It didn't sound like you at all, and it completely broke my heart. Those words and your voice will forever be embedded in my head, and I'm so sorry I didn't come home to see you one last time.

You were truly one of a kind, and I think the worst part is that absolutely no one compares to how selfless and compassionate you were to everyone around you. It's hard for other people to understand, first of all, because our family was abnormally close and, second, people don't act that way nowadays. You grew up in one of the hardest times, during the Great Depression, without any parents by the age of 13, and without much to even get by with, and yet you would still light up even for the littlest things.

Sometimes I never understand why God does what He does but I guess I can find peace in knowing you are finally with all your brothers, sisters, Aunt Mimi and Uncle Tom (your best buddies), and your wife. I will always be your "little blue eyes" and I can't wait to see you again one day. I love you so much too, Papa.

Always,
Jaimee xoxoxo

My good friend Sarah also had a dream about my father, and she shared this with me:

January 17, 2019, Text message:

Good morning my friend! I thought about this. Actually, I dreamt about it. You do know why you are being reunited with your siblings at this point in your life, right? Because when your parents, aunts and uncles got to Heaven, they met some of your birth family and they are helping you on this journey from above. I know you miss them very much, but they are always with you.

Remember that.

Love ya, xoxo Sarah

Chapter Thirty-Nine:
It Was Always You and Me

Dear Dad,

Looking back your mind can play tricks on you. I see a figure of myself, and flashback to sitting on my bedroom floor, back up against my door, arms around my knees, head buried and crying my eyes out. I was maybe 10 years old, at most. During those awful times, those fights, the screaming and hollering of my mother as she railed, you tried your best to reason with a drug-addicted wife.

I see my form as a child, cowering, crying, and waiting for that hell to end. How you endured Mom's sickness I will never know.

Flash forward decades later. I am sitting on the cold cement step, the entrance to our house, on the garage side, just sitting, still cowering. Crying. I am taking a break from seeing Mom, who is now so deteriorated, half blind, constantly in and out of the hospital. I must come sit out here and take a break from the horrific reality. She is inside, dying. We don't know this, for sure, yet we do.

Years of abuse to her body, heart failure, diabetes, and more have all taken their toll. I come outside because it's too much. I am alone again. No siblings, no friends, no other family. Just me, sitting there on the cold cement step. I don't know what to do because there is nothing I can do.

You stay inside, of course, her constant caretaker.

Eventually, I'll have to go back in to face the nightmare circus. The merry-go-round of hospitals is about to begin, again. Not sure what round we are on, but this will be our last round with Mom, at least.

It is summer of 2003. Maybe it's June. I don't know anymore.

She will die just days after her birthday, in July. The 17th—which has always been my unlucky number, guess I should have predicted that.

That last round is so exhausting, sad, and vicious for us all. I just remember running up to the hospital on her birthday, July 12th, balloons in hand, a small cake. She is lying in the bed. I bring the kids up to see her somewhere during this time. Maybe on her actual birthday. She is half delirious, sleeping a lot. Her heart is failing.

You took the small cake out that I brought when I bring the kids there. Mom can't eat it. You courageously suggest, along with Aunt Millie, I think, that we sing Happy Birthday to "Nannie" and cut the cake and serve it to the kids. I don't even think she wakes up or realizes it's her birthday. Aunt Millie and Uncle Tom come and Rick is there. There are unopened birthday cards piled up on her hospital tray table.

We are back at Rochester General. She is in hospice on the 5th floor.

After a few days of friends and family who stop by to say their goodbyes, on a Wednesday we all stay as long as we can, and then we leave her with her shallow breathing. You call it a "death rattle." I say goodbye over and over, and then I leave. As I walk out of her room, I think back over all the years, and what a long, incredibly, impossibly difficult struggle it's been for her and for all of us. She's leaving, but we are not and have to carry on.

Days before she dies, she tells me how much she loved me, and the kids, Dad, Rick, and all the family.

She also teases me and tells me about some people that she knows have caused me a lot of heartache and pain and tells me, shrugging, not to worry about it, and that "they just don't know what love is." She assures me that although she's leaving, I have Rick and the kids and that I will be okay. She tells me, she's sorry for all the pain she caused, and she blames it on "menopause." I find this internally hilarious and revolting at the same time, and it's the last bomb she will drop on me. MENOPAUSE? That's the best she can come up with for the HELL we went through?

Oh well. The joke is on us. She just cannot, even now, really admit to herself or to us that this was addiction.

I make my peace with it, although not in that moment. I love her dearly, and always and still do. It is what it is, and there's once again, nothing I can do about any of this.

You are exhausted and I think we stop by Aunt Millie's that night, in July, and she feeds us all.

We go home. At midnight, I get the call. It's always at midnight.

What I do not know but can only imagine, was that this was just the beginning of my learning to say goodbye. To let you all go. To watch you all get sick. To take care of everyone.

More hospitals, doctors, surgeries, pills, medicine, emergencies that were never ending followed. Mom died, and as bad as that was, this was just the beginning for Rick and I and the girls. Waiting. Always waiting, praying, crying, trying, caretaking, loving, hoping. Asking questions until the very end.

Seeing the faces of endless doctors, nurses, and walking the halls of all the local hospitals, the story repeated itself. It was the same routine with each of you. All of us desperately trying to cling to hope, keep our humor and our sanity. One by one, I watched you each fall. In the end, it was like dominoes.

I did my best. I know you knew that. So did Aunt Millie and Uncle Tom. Feeling lost and alone, but no one could save you all. I couldn't. Everyone tried to tell me; you were all old; it was your time. But it really didn't matter, did it? For you were mine and I was yours.

All that suffering. But I would do it all again, in a heartbeat. Take care of you all as you always took care of me.

When I left Mom's room that night, I felt the echo of her spirit behind me. I felt like she was saying goodbye, and I felt her spirit trailing behind me for a short distance, as I exited the corridor of the hospital, but not for the last time. It was only the beginning of many more thank you's, I love you's, and goodbyes.

I know that your resilience, your character, your lessons, your spirit lives in my heart every day. Dad, you, and the others taught me life is beautiful and worth living, despite the worst pain and struggles and to never give up, not ever. I don't plan on it. I love you forever and a day. You and me, we triumphed, didn't we, Dad? Against sickness, pain, and death. You can't ask for more than that. Thanks for teaching me to persist and be a survivor. We won. We all did. I want you to know we are all good and praying for all of you, always, as you all continue to watch over all of us.

Until we meet again...

Your loving daughter,
Diane

Epilogue: Dear Rose

I never did get to meet my birth mother, Rose, even after learning her identity from genealogist, David Guentner, and after meeting my sister, Karen, in 2016. I thought a lot about the things I had learned about her, her personality, her life, and her circumstances. I then thought to myself, why not write her a letter? My parents had often expressed to me, their gratitude to her for making the decision to give me up for adoption. Although she is gone and I will never meet her, this is what I would say to her, if I could. Hopefully, my words are delivered to heaven, instead.

ROSE ARGENTINA
43 Austin St.
"Sweeter than the roses of
May."

A high school yearbook photo of my biological mother, Rose Argentina. It's also the first picture I ever saw of her when I discovered her identity in 2016 when I was 53. It was a shock to see a picture of my birth mom for the very first time.

IT WAS ALWAYS YOU AND ME

Dear Rose:

I want to thank you for bringing me into this world and giving me the opportunity to have a wonderful life, with the most wonderful parents my soul could have chosen, because I have now learned this is what some religions actually believe to be true. It is believed that our souls chose our parents long before we arrive on this planet. If that is the case, you not only did a very unselfish thing in giving me up for adoption, but after your decision was made, perhaps I, too, had a say in choosing the best parents I could have ever wanted or hoped for.

I never really felt the need to search for you or for anyone. This was not out of any bitterness or anger towards you. No, I never felt the need to search for you or to meet you because I already had the best family. I had won the lottery in this regard, and I always knew that.

Now, if I am completely honest, was I curious from time to time about who you were or who my biological father was? Of course, as I am only human. I wondered who I looked like, and I wondered what kind of person you were. As I grew older, if the topic of my adoption came up or my feelings about adoption, only then did it force me to give any thought to it.

I felt pressured more, by people, curious to know how I felt or why I wasn't more curious. When I was asked about being adopted, I would pause and try to come up with answers that would satisfy others and could tell they seemed disappointed that I did not have anything earth shattering to report to them. I was satisfied, and they could not understand that, or expected something different or "more" from me, but I didn't have it to give to them.

There were those times, of course, when I thought to myself, "Why did I have to be the person someone chose to give away to another family?" And, "Who were these people who created me, and why have they never looked for ME?"

There were even times, I would be in large crowds, like at a concert, or a baseball game, and think to myself, "Could my mother be here, and I wouldn't even know?" I never wondered about my biological father, curiously. Not ever. I didn't even think about HAVING a biological father, which is kind of funny, and I have no idea why that is. I didn't feel sad, I just wondered where you were, or if our paths had crossed, and I wouldn't even know it if they did. It was an odd feeling, really, knowing you existed somewhere "out there."

I realize now, going through all that you did, in 1955, giving up another child previous to me, and then again, giving me up in 1962, how incredibly hard that must have been. The times were not forgiving, and your strict Italian Catholic upbringing must have made it a million times harder for you. You had no support, I found out your family was very hard on you, so hard it caused you mental anguish enough to cause you mental breakdowns over this. I also learned that your own mother had died when you were only 11 years old.

My parents always told me I was "chosen" from a young age, that they loved me, as my entire extended family did, beyond words. They said I was the dream that had come true for them. Their words, when I was little, didn't register fully. As I grew up, the meaning of those beautiful words filled in the spaces of my heart, and blurred and erased most of my curiosity for I had all I needed. The bond I shared with my parents and family grew to unimaginable proportions. I knew I was closer to my parents than many biological children are to their parents. I was also aware many envied the wonderful family I had and the love we shared.

I always felt enormous responsibility to try to make my parents proud for all the love and sacrifices they gave to me and made for me. I wasn't perfect, but I tried to be a good girl, daughter, and student. I hope I succeeded in making them proud and tried to take care of all my family in their old age.

They are all gone, now, as are you and my biological Dad.

So, while I will never get to meet you, Rose, or thank you in person, I want you to know I did learn some things about you from a cousin I met and from your sister-in-law, that I got to meet, and, also, from information from the NYS Adoption Registry.

I learned that you played piano. You loved to dance. You were a high school cheerleader. You were the "life of the party," had a petite figure and a beautiful smile, that "lit up the room." I learned that you would help anyone in need. Most importantly, I learned that you were strong and a good person.

I want you to know, my family was always grateful to you. I am forever indebted to you for giving me the gift of life, and I pray that you eventually found happiness and peace.

Love,
Your daughter, Diane

About the Author

Diane DiProspero-Cook grew up in Rochester in Upstate New York. She and her husband Rick live with two adorable pups, a Shorkie and a Havapoo. They have two grown daughters. Their oldest daughter is married, with her master's degree from Utica College and works in the field of health care and medical coding. Their youngest daughter is a Niagara University graduate engaged to be married and is employed as a nurse in the PACU department, currently.

Diane is, at long last, finishing her bachelor's degree in English literature, from SUNY Brockport College. She enjoys reading, cooking, biking, working out, traveling, theatre, and spending time with family and friends.

It Was Always You and Me is her first book, a memoir and tribute honoring her father, Joseph, and her entire adoptive family. She is especially close to and cherishes her many wonderful cousins and close friends. Recently, she was thrilled to find and connect with several newfound biological siblings.

She hopes this story will touch your heart and encourage all those who grew up in families whose loved ones battled addiction and the children who became adult survivors.

Acknowledgements

To Rick, thank you for always supporting all my dreams. Without you, I could not have done this and so much more. We are quite the team, no? This life has been a wild ride, and I don't know where I would be without you. Thank you for always having my back and for all the love and sacrifices you have made for me and all the family. There is no one like you! I love you, forever grateful to you—my hero!

To my kids, Shannon and Jaimee, and their spouses, Mark and Justin, I love you all. You guys are the best family ever. This story is for you guys to help you preserve all the memories and love from the family. I hope it helps you understand me and them better and always keep them close in your heart and never forget them. They all loved you fiercely, as do Dad and I—always remember that.

To my sister, Karen, you are the dream that came true, the sibling I wished for, much love. I hope you are as happy to have found me as I was to have found you. Here's to more years of sisterly love and making memories. Love you so much.

To all my new siblings: Karen (yes "another" Karen), Janet, Kevin, Beverly, and Ken. I am so glad I found you; I hope we continue to get to know one another. Thanks for accepting me and for your love and kindness. I hope we get to make many nice memories going forward. Love you all.

To all my cousins, friends, and neighbors, too numerous to name but you know who you are, thank you for being in my life, for whatever role you have played in my life. I see you and I love and appreciate you all with all my heart—you put such joy and sparkle into my life. I cherish you all, and hope you enjoy my story. Looking forward to many more years of spending time and making more memories together.

To Troy Lambert, I thank you! I appreciate your help more than you know. You are a wizard! Thank you so very much. Without you my dream would not be a reality!

A special thank you to Mary Farone, Ph.D., for all your help and work and for inspiring and believing in me.

To Elly Stevens, you are a godsend. I can't thank you enough for all you've done. I so appreciate you; you are simply the best! How can I ever thank you enough?

To Elle J. Rossi, for the beautiful cover artwork, thank you!

To Dana Long and Suzanne Blessing for all your help, it means so much, and I could not have done this alone.

To Joseph, "Dad," you have and always will remain my inspiration, my true "North." I know you are watching over me, Dad. This book is for you, it is our story. I hope you are proud of me; I know you always told me you were. I will never forget the man you were, your struggles and the love and enormous sacrifices you made for me and Mom, and really everyone you knew. I will love you forever.

> *Never forgotten, and*
> *until we meet again,*
> *"Your Diane"*

Made in the USA
Monee, IL
06 November 2021

81548026R00167